INSIGHT COMPACT GUIDES

BRUS

Compact Guide: Brussels details the attractions of the former weavers' town that has reinvented itself as the cosmopolitan capital of the European Union. The book savours its elegant architecture, surveys its great galleries and museums, and samples its superb cuisine.

This is just one title in *Apa Publications'* new series of pocket-sized, easy-to-use guidebooks intended for the independent-minded traveller. Based on an award-winning formula pioneered in Germany, *Compact Guides* pride themselves on being up-to-date and authoritative. They are in essence mini travel encyclopedias, designed to be comprehensive yet portable, both readable and reliable.

Star Attractions

An instant reference to some of Brussel's most popular tourist attractions to help you on your way.

Grand' Place p15

Museum of Older Art p20

Notre-Dame-du-Bon-Secours p30

Atomium p43

Waterloo and Panorama Museum p53

Cathedral of Our Dear Lady p60

Rubens House p61

Ghent Altarpiece p65

Manneken Pis p25

Leuven Town Hall p67

Abbey of St Gertrude p68

BRUSSELS

Brussels – The Capital of Europe

Mention Brussels, and what will most immediately spring to mind is the increasingly key role that the city plays in the lives and destinies of millions of Europeans. But this is no accident of history, for Brussels, today's capital designate of Europe, has always been at the forefront of developments. In the days when the Low Countries were in French hands, then in Spanish, then in Austrian, Brussels was always the chosen capital of 'the Netherlands'; even after becoming the capital of the independent Kingdom of Belgium in 1830, the city maintained a strongly European identity.

The latter half of this century has seen Brussels consolidate its position, first becoming, in 1958, headquarters of the European Economic Community (EEC) and the European Atomic Energy Community (EURATOM). A year before these two bodies, and the European Coal and Steel Community, merged to become the European Community in 1967, the city became home to the headquarters of the Permanent Council of the North Atlantic Treaty Organisation (NATO), which moved here from France. Due to the concentration of important European institutions in Brussels, the city now ranks third world-wide, behind Paris and London, as a centre for congresses.

Although the poets and thinkers, artists and merchants it once attracted have now been largely superseded by the planners of the European Community and NATO, Brussels remains a thriving place, where citizens not only of Europe but of the world can feel at home. As the capital of Europe, the profile presented by the city evolves from year to year. In addition to its venerable and noteworthy sights dating from past centuries, including its magnificent market square, the Grand' Place, Brussels also presents an increasingly modern face to visitors as ever more new office blocks are erected to meet the demands of the city's emergent role.

Brewery Museum, Grand' Place

Brussels' modern face

Location and size

Brussels, the capital of the kingdom of Belgium and the province of Brabant, is located at 50.8° north longitude and 4.4° east latitude, placing it almost at the centre of the country. The northwest boundary of the country is a coastline of 67km (42 miles). Belgium is bordered to the north by Holland, to the east by Germany, to the southeast by Luxembourg and to the south and southwest by France.

The city centre is contained within a mere 3,292ha (8,134 acres) while metropolitan Brussels sprawls over 16,000ha (39,535 acres). Because parts of Brussels are situated on hills along the Senne valley, the altitude of the city ranges from 15–100m (49–328ft) above sea level. For

Parliament Building

this reason, a distinction is made between the lower city, which includes the Old Town, and the upper city which affords a lovely panorama of the lower-lying neighbourhoods. The downtown area, enclosed by a 7-km (4-mile) long boulevard ring which follows the path of the former city wall, is becoming more and more a commercial and business centre as the residential population moves out of the city. It is here that the offices of the Belgian government as well as the parliament are found, while most of the European government offices are located further east, between the ring and the Cinquantenaire Park, in the Léopold Quarter.

Economy

Because of its central location, Brussels is an important crossroads for Belgium, and indeed for all Europe. The Bruxelles/Brussel International Airport, located 10km (6 miles) northeast of the city in Zaventem, makes the city an important transportation centre. As for motorway traffic, the Belgian capital looks somewhat like a spider in a net, serving as the hub for routes leading into the city from Liège, Namur, Charleroi, Mons, Ghent and Antwerp. These spokes are all joined in a huge beltway which encircles Brussels.

Crossroads of Europe

6

Several international railway lines also lead through Brussels, making it a central junction for one of the world's most densely concentrated railway systems. These lines play an important role in linking Great Britain and Germany as well as France and Holland. To make this network even more efficient, a 6-track underground rail system was built in 1952 to link the former end stations in the northern and southern parts of the city.

Whereas water transportation in Brussels is relatively insignificant for tourism, the city's role in shipping can-

Canal trade

not be ignored. The Charleroi Canal links the capital with the industrial regions in the south of Belgium while the Willebroek Canal provides access to the Brussels inland harbour on the Scheldt river, leading to Antwerp and the open sea.

As the Belgian financial capital, Brussels is the seat of the national bank as well as of numerous industrial and commercial enterprises. In this vein, the textile industry, with its production of wool and upholstery materials as well as Brussels lace, is just as worthy of mention as the larger operations. Many of the latter are international, including the metal, electrical, chemical and cardboard industries. Rubber goods, machines, matches, clothing, food, beer and laundry detergent are also manufactured in Brussels.

Brussels lace

Population, language and culture

Situated only a few kilometres north of the linguistic border between Flemings in the north and Walloons in the south, Brussels is officially bilingual. The visitor will immediately notice that signs and street names, as well as all the city districts, are labelled in both Flemish and French. Speakers of the French (Walloon) language, however, are definitely in the majority.

Bilingual signs

7

The city centre of Brussels, strictly defined, has only about 145,000 inhabitants. However, a unique municipal government structure unites 19 semi-autonomous communities with the centre to form greater Brussels, with a population of over a million. The high proportion of foreigners (almost 23 percent) gives the city a distinctly cosmopolitan air. In recent years, a substantial Islamic community, made up of people originating from North Africa and Turkey, has developed.

Brussels' significance as the cultural centre of Belgium is evidenced by the location here of the Royal Academy, founded in 1772, the Free University (1834) and the Polytechnic Institute (1873). Additionally, a number of art academies and institutes of higher learning, the Albert I Library and more than 30 small museums and collections ranging in subject matter from the Royal Museum of Art and History to the exhibition Pioneering in Medicine, testify to the city's status as a cultural focal point. Among the more than 30 theatres, experimental stages and cultural centres located here, the National Opera plays by far the most important role.

Enjoying some culture

The boroughs

As already mentioned, the community of Brussels is only one relatively small part of greater Brussels, also known as the Région Bruxelloise. This conurbation includes 19 semi-autonomous *communes*, in addition to Brussels itself (*see Map page 9*). These former suburbs are now so integrated with the centre that greater Brussels today appears as a united cityscape.

The centre of Brussels includes, in addition to the downtown area within the boulevard ring and the adjacent residential area of Quartier Léopold to the east, the sections of Laeken, Over Heembeek, Neder Heembeek and Haren to the northeast.

Centenaire Hall, Heysel

To the northwest is Heysel with its royal domain and World Exhibition site and, to the south, the wooded park Bois de la Cambre. (Brussels has more parks and green, open spaces than most European cities, providing welcome respite for busy office workers). Visitors exploring the city would never notice that they have crossed from Brussels or Brussels II, as the northern part of town is known, into one of the adjoining boroughs. It only becomes apparent in cases where one must deal with a local government agency.

The following nine boroughs form the inside ring around Brussels: the narrow St-Josse-ten-Noode (with the Botanical Garden) to the northeast; adjacent to that lies Schaerbeek (North Station); Etterbeek is to the east; Ixelles (with several museums) to the southeast, a borough divided by the Brussels corridor leading to Bois de la Cambre; St Gilles (South station) to the south; Anderlecht (with the Canal de Charleroi and the Erasmus House), as well as Molenbeek-St Jean and Koekelberg (which has a basilica) to the west and Jette to the northwest.

The outer ring of boroughs includes: Evere (with the NATO headquarters and the main cemetery) in the east; Woluwe-St Lambert and Woluwe-St Pierre (Woluwe Park) also to the east; Auderghem (where the Val Duchesse Abbey is situated) to the south; Watermael-Boitsfort (containing the northeastern part of the Soignes Woods), Uccle (home to the Observatory) as well as Forest (with Duden Park and St Denis Abbey) also to the south and Berchem-St Agathe and Ganshoren to the northwest.

Suburbs of Brussels

Only a few of the suburbs, situated further outside the city, are of any interest to the visitor. Starting in the east of Brussels and going clockwise, they include: Kraainem at the Brussels East junction of the ring and the Liège/Leuven motorway; Tervuren with the informative Museum of Central Africa; Beersel with its moated castle; Drogenbos and Ruisbroek where the Senne river and the Charleroi Canal first reach the city limits; Grand Bigard with a castle which is now a museum; Strombeek-Bever and, directly to the north, Meise, worth visiting for the Domäne Bouchout (Botanical Garden) as well as Grimbergen with an abbey of the same name.

Botanical Garden

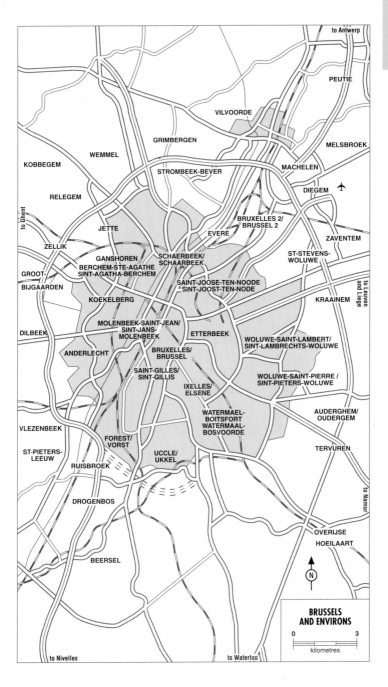

BRUSSELS
AND ENVIRONS

0   3

kilometres

Historical Highlights

According to legend, Brussels was founded in the 6th century by Saint Géry on an island in the Senne river. It was first documented in AD966 in a chronicle of Emperor Otto I which referred to it as Bruoscella ('Settlement in the Marshes'), the seat of many counts from the region. Several islands in the Senne, located at the site of today's city centre, were declared military outposts and in 977 a small wooden fort was constructed on one of them. In 979 Charles, Duke of Lorraine, made it his residence.

The real development of the city began in the 11th century when the later-to-be Duke of Brabant settled on the Coudenberg, the site of today's Place Royale/Koningsplein and surrounding streets. Brussels' location on an important trade route of the time, between Cologne and Bruges, ensured a long era of prosperity throughout the 12th and 13th century. Brussels grew to become one of the major towns in the duchy of Brabant. Its economy was largely based on the manufacture of luxury fabrics, which made their way to fairs in Paris, Venice and elsewhere. Business and municipal matters were almost exclusively controlled by a handful of wealthy merchant dynastieswho had grown rich and powerful from the cloth trade. Their abuse of power led to a number of popular uprisings during medieval times.

Around 1100 The first fortification walls are built in Brussels.

1379–83 After Brussels' occupation by the troops of the Count of Flanders, a new, 6-km (4-mile) long city wall with 74 towers and six gates is constructed. The line of the wall, shaped like a coat of arms, is almost identical to that of the inner boulevard ring surrounding the city centre today.

1402 Construction of the Town Hall begins in the market place.

1421 A popular uprising leads to a fairer system of government, with local powers divided between the patrician families and the emergent guilds of craftsmen and other workers.

1430–77 Philip the Good becomes ruler of Brabant and Brussels. The Burgundian period sees Brussels become the favourite residential city of the Duke of Burgundy in the Low Countries, which constitute a rich centre of art and culture.

1455 The city has a population of 40,000.

1477 Mary of Burgundy grants permission to dig the Willebroek Canal, a lateral channel to the Senne.

1521 The Humanist Desiderius Erasmus of Rotterdam moves into his house in Anderlecht near Brussels.

1522 The treaty between Charles V and his brother Ferdinand, dividing the great Habsburg empire between the German and the Spanish lines, is signed in Brussels.

Two Lutheran preachers are burned at the stake in Brussels; their martyrdom strengthens the forces of the Reformation in the city.

1531 Emperor Charles V chooses Brussels over Mechelen as the capital of the Habsburg Netherlands. Mary of Hungary and Margaret of Parma also later reside here.

1561 Completion of today's Sea Canal, named Willebroek Canal (see also 1477), linking Brussels to the Scheldt and thus to the North Sea; thereafter, three large harbour basins are dug in the northern part of the city.

1566 The first revolt of the Netherlands against its Spanish sovereign breaks out in Brussels.

1568 The Counts Egmont and Hoorn, leaders of the resistance movement, are executed in the market place.

1579–85 After the southern provinces of the Low Countries (which included modern-day Belgium) separate from the northern provinces (now the Netherlands), Brussels returns to the Roman Catholic fold.

1598–1633 The reign of Archduke Albert and Isabella. The Counter-Reformation leaves its mark on the city landscape with the construction of a series of fine churches in the Italian-Flemish baroque style.

1695 The French, under Marshal Villeroi, bombard Brussels; hundreds of buildings are destroyed by fire, including the various craft headquarters. The numerous French wars against Spain and Austria have already adversely affected Brussels, hampering its prosperity, but after this catastrophe new guild halls are built, the architectural landmarks now surrounding the market place, or Grand' Place.

1794 Following the Brabant revolt against the government of Austrian Emperor Joseph II, the Belgian principalities are annexed to France. The French revolutionary government names Brussels as capital of the Dyle Departement.

1815 Napoleon is defeated just outside Brussels, at Waterloo.

1815–30 Brussels and the Hague alternate as the seat of the monarchy after the Congress of Vienna orders the merging of the territory of today's Belgium and the Netherlands, creating the United Kingdom of the Netherlands.

1829–36 The Willebroek Canal is dredged for the first time to enable passage for larger ships (also see 1902).

1830 The Belgian revolution erupts in Brussels. Belgium declares its independence and Brussels is chosen as the capital.

1831 Leopold of Saxe-Coburg arrives with great ceremony in Brussels and becomes the first Belgian king, taking the name Leopold I. Brussels becomes the seat of the Belgian monarchy.

1846 The Galerie Saint-Hubert (*see page 36*) is built near the Brussels market place. It is the first glass-covered shopping arcade in Europe. Seven neighbouring communities are incorporated into Brussels, forming an Agglomération which is later joined by 11 other bordering communities.

1897 Brussels World Exhibition in Cinquantenaire Museum and Exhibition Palace.

1902–14 and **1918–22** Dredging of the Willebroek Canal, after which it can accommodate ships with a draught of up to 5.8m (19ft).

1910 World Exhibition held in Brussels in the Cinquantenaire Palace.

1914–18 World War I. Adolphe de Max, the burgomaster of Brussels, acquires fame for his resistance to the German occupying forces.

1935 World Exhibition in Brussels/Heysel.

May 1940 Brussels falls to the invading German army. The city suffers no extensive physical damage, but is subjected to harsh terms of occupation. Leopold III is interned in Laeken Castle. As in World War I, Germany tries to divide the nation by supporting partisans of Flemish autonomy.

September 1944 The city is liberated by the British and the legitimate Belgian government returns to its capital from London.

1951 Leopold III abdicates in favour of his son Baudouin.

1952 Construction of an underground railway connection between the North and South stations, both of which were previously terminus stations. Construction of a central train station to the east of the Grand' Place and establishment of an inner city rail service with three downtown stations.

1958 International World Exhibition at Heysel fair grounds. The fair's landmark is the Atomium, and the event helps to boost the weakened post-war economy. Brussels becomes the seat of the European Economic Community (EEC).

1967 NATO headquarters moves from France to Belgium. The new location is to the northeast of Brussels along the motorway connecting Brussels and Zaventem.

1972 Great Britain joins the Common Market, along with Denmark and Ireland.

1989 In the reorganisation of the Belgian state, Brussels becomes the Capital Region, alongside Flanders and Wallonia.

1991 Early parliamentary elections result in a breakthrough for the environmentalist party in the French-speaking Walloon region and a resurgence of the right-wing radical party in the Dutch-language region of Flanders.

1993 King Baudouin dies on 31 July and is succeeded by his brother Albert.

1995 The provinces of Flemish Brabant and Walloon Brabant are created from the old province of Brabant, giving Belgium a total of ten provinces.

BRUSSELS CITY CENTRE

0 _____ 750
metres

N

12

To Koekelberg and Anderlecht

Church of St John
Church of St Catherine
Place de Ninove
BOURSE
Stock Exchange
Grand' Place
Town Hall
Church of Our Lady
Manneken Pis
Pl. Rouppe
Church of Our Lady of the Chapel
Gare du midi
Palace of Justice
Museum der altsächsichen Wohlfahrt

RUE PIERS
R. de Rhaucourt
Charbonnages
BD DU 9 E DE LIGNE
QUAI DU COMMERCE
BD
BD
CHAUSSEE DE GAND
R. de Menin
R. d Menin
Ch. de Merode
R. de l'Avenir
Quai des
Rue du Canal
R. d. Gr. Hospice
R. D. L. VIERGE NOIRE
ANSPACH
RUE DU FLANDRE
RUE A. DANSAERT
BD DE BARTHELEMY
Quai du
Hainaut
Quai
Seine
Rue des Fabriques
de
ARTEVELDE
R. D. MARCHE
R. D.
MALUS
Rue de Flandre
Rue de Pierres
R. A. VANDENPEEREBOOM
R. D. INDEPENDANCE
R. de Elephant
des Quatre Vents
Mariemont
de l'Industrie
Heyvaert
CH. DE NINOVE
R. D. BIRMINGHAM
Quai
de Liverpool
Rue de
Rue
BOULEVARD
RUE VAN
BD ANSPACH
RUE DU MIDI
RUE DU LOMBARD
R. ROPSY CHANDRON
CHAUSSEE DE MONS
BOULEVARD POINCARE
BOULEVARD M. LEMONNIER LAAN
Rue des Foulons
RUE DU
Pl. Rouppe
Rue de Borgens
Rue d' Alexiens
Rue de l'Etuve
Rue d' Anderlecht
AVENUE CLEMENCEAU
Rue de la Clinique
R. DE FIENNES
Rue Broigniez
Rue de la Révision
Rue Bara
Rue d'Instructions
Bd de la Révision
VEEARTSEN STR
Bara
RUE DE FRANCE
AVENUE FONSNY
Gare du midi
R. de Deux Gares
R. d' Angleterre
AVE DE LA PORTE
MIDI
AVE DE STALINGRAD
Rue des Tanneurs
Rue du Miroir
Rue de Brigittines
BLAES
RUE
HAUTE
Rue aux Laines
Rue Jourdan
BOULEVARD DE WATERLOO
AVE D. L. TOISON
AVE V.-JASPER
Ch. de Forest
R. Feron
Ch. de HAL
R. d' Poincon

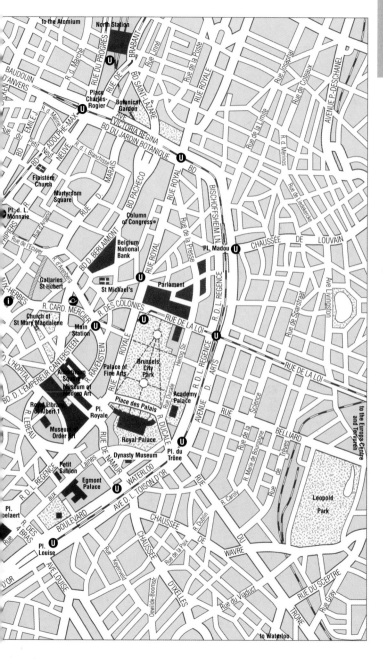

Route 1

Around the ★★★ Grand' Place

As a matter of course every visitor to this city is drawn to the centre, to the Town Hall Square, known in Walloon as Grand' Place and in Flemish as Grote Markt.

This is, without a doubt, not only the focal point of the city but also a superb example of a medieval city centre. It is, quite simply, one of the most lovely squares in the world. The harmony of today's baroque facades is due to the solidarity shown by the guilds during the period following the firebombing by the French troops in 1695. Not only did they spontaneously agree to reconstruct the square in its former style but they also carried out the work in an expeditious manner.

In former times the Grand' Place was the commercial, political and cultural centre of Brussels, a role which it has, over time, unfortunately sacrificed. Today, although the main offices of the industrial giants, housed in modern glass structures, are still located inside the 7-km (4-mile) long boulevard ring, they are scattered throughout the entire downtown area. The same is true for the government offices. And so today the Grand' Place is dominated by crowds of tourists from around the world. Arriving mainly in groups, they listen fleetingly to the tour guide's brief description of the square before hurrying on to the next sight. Those few who manage to linger a bit longer here, retreating from the tumult perhaps to the refuge of one of the coffee-houses, might be able to call to the mind's eye an image of what this square once was, of life before the hustle and bustle of modern times.

Tourist in the square

15

The most prominent building is the ★★ **Town Hall** (Hôtel de Ville/Stadhuis). This is one of the best-preserved secular structures from the Gothic period. The larger portion of the building, to the left, was built from 1402 to 1404. The smaller section, on the right, was added in the years after 1444. The tower, adorned with a statue of St Michael, the patron saint of Brussels, was completed in 1454 and restored in 1897. The top of the tower (400 steps up) offers a spectacular view of the city. The entire rear portion of the complex was rebuilt after the French attack and was not finally completed until the 18th century. The facade of the Town Hall is decorated with numerous statues, which include several interesting specimens of 14th- and 15th-century Brussels sculpture

The Town Hall

In addition to the facade, interesting attractions are the two **fountains** (from 1715) in the courtyard, symbolising the Maas and Scheldt rivers, as well as several large rooms inside the building where the so-called Brussels Tapestries are housed. Originally appointed in neoclassical

One of the fountains

Town Hall facade

The Manneken Pis

style, the main Council Chamber was redesigned in the Gothic idiom in 1868. Tapestries adorning the walls depict the city's principal traditional crafts and the guilds which practised them. The wall hangings were created between 1875–81 in Mechelen. Former presidents of the municipal council are represented as gilt bronze statues in front of the columns, and the windows illustrate the coats of arms of noble Brussels families.

It is possible to walk around the entire Town Hall complex following the Rue Charles Buis/Karel Buisstraat (further along this road is the famous statue of Manneken Pis, *see Route 3, page 25*), the Rue de l'Amigo/Vruntstraat (rear facade) and the Rue de la Tête d'Or/Guldenhoofdstraat, ending up back at the Grand' Place, right next to the Town Hall.

Here seven old ★ **guild halls** are crowded closely together along the square. Some of their historic names, listed here, have been changed throughout the centuries and thus do not always correspond to the names displayed today. House No 7 is the Grocers' House, sometimes also called the Fox House owing to the figure above the door. No 6 is the Mariners' House (1696) with a gable designed as a ship's stern. The next house, No 5, is the Archers' House (1691), also known as the House of the She-Wolf, based on the figure of the Capitoline she-wolf with Remus and Romulus. Note the gilt Phoenix on the gable. House No 4 is the Joiners' and Coopers' House (built in 1644, restored in 1697). At No 3 is the House of the Lard Dealers (also constructed in 1644 and rebuilt in 1697) and finally, at No 1/2 is the Bakers' House (1697) with a bust of the Spanish king Charles II.

The facade of the building opposite the Town Hall, on the other end of the square, is divided into three sectors. In the centre is the King's House, flanked on either side by more guild halls. Across the Rue au Beurre/Boterstraat, adjacent to house No 1 are, among others, the Oaktree House (No 37) and the Peacock House (No 35).

The **King's House** (Maison du Roi), also originally called the Bread House (Broodhuis) when it served as the bakers' guild hall, was reconstructed in its present form between 1873 and 1895, in an imitation of its original 16th-century style. It was first built between 1515 and 1525 but was destroyed when the French attacked the city in 1695. In 1568, Count Egmont and Count Hoorn, the celebrated leaders of the revolt against the Catholic policies pursued by Philip II within the Spanish Netherlands, were held in the King's House before their execution on the Grand' Place.

In the past the King's House has been the seat of various courts and a prison, but today it houses the Brussels **Municipal Museum** (Musée Communal de la Ville de Bruxelles/Stedelijk Museum van Brussel), opened in 1887. The main attraction of this museum is the collection of 26 paintings donated to the city by an Englishman, John Waterloo Wilson. These works include the *Allegory of the United Provinces* by N Verkolie, *Still Life with Food* by Willem Claesz Heda and *Portrait of a Clergyman*, attributed to the artist Josse van Cleve. The museum's collection also presents a first-class historical documentation with statues of the prophets originally in the Town Hall (late 14th-century), two Brussels retables (altarpieces from the late 15th and early 16th century), four 16th-century Brussels tapestries including *The Legend of Notre Dame du Sablon* (attributed to Barend van Orley), the painting *Wedding Procession* by Pieter Brueghel the Elder as well as the most complete collection of Brussels ceramics, dating from the period 1710–1845.

The Municipal Museum

The museum has a separate section called the **Wardrobe of Manneken Pis** (Garderobe de Manneke Pis/De Klerenverzameling van Manneke Pis; *see page 25*). It houses a collection of over 450 different articles of clothing, costumes and uniforms which have been donated to the city since the 18th century for this renowned figure, Brussels' oldest citizen and a city landmark. This department also contains numerous documents about the city's historical development.

On either side of the King's House is a small alley leading to the Rue du Marché aux Herbes/Grasmarkt, location of the TIB (Tourist Information Brussels) where multilingual hostesses are available to assist tourists with information about the city. Adjacent to the King's House are, among others, the Painters' House (Nos 27–26), the Tai-

The Brewers' House

The House of the Swan

lors' House (No 25) with a bust of St Barbe, their patron saint, and the House of the Old City Scales (No 24).

At the other side of the Rue de la Colline/Heuvelstraat, which branches off from the next corner of the square, is the **House of the Dukes of Brabant**, dating from 1698. This building forms one end of the rectangular market place. Consisting of six former guild halls, it was named for the busts of the dukes which adorn the capitals of the Ionic columns along the facade. At the end of this row, the Rue de Chapeliers/Hoedenmakerstraat leads off the square. Across that street is the Town Hall facade which houses, in addition to the Town Hall itself, more guild halls, including: No 12, the House of the Three Colours (1699); No 11, the House of the Rose (1702), No 10, the Brewers' House (with a gilt equestrian statue of Charles of Lorraine); No 9, the **House of the Swan**, the former guild hall of the butchers (1698) (once the home of Karl Marx and now one of the city's most elegant and expensive restaurants); and No 8, the Star House, rebuilt in 1897.

The Brewers' House is the location of the **Brussels Brewery Museum** (Musée de la Brasserie/Brouwerijmuseum). It is set up as an old brewery with a complete collection of everything necessary for the brewing of beer (cellar, kegs and implements used in former times as well as beer steins). Beside the brewery is a lively pub where the visitor has the opportunity to sample the Brussels beer at the site where it is made.

The stroll around the Grand' Place is now complete. A return visit to the square in the evening is to be recommended, when the illumination of the buildings gives the square an even more magical glow.

Route 2

Chapel of St Mary Magdalene – Albertinum – ★★ Museums of Old and Modern Art – Academy Palace – Royal Palace – Palace of Fine Arts

Because of the Grand' Place's important role and its central location – it is situated close to the main station as well as to three underground stations – all of the walking tours through the downtown area (*Routes 2–6*) begin and end at this point. The first route leaves the square via the Rue de la Colline/Heuvelstraat and leads southeast towards the large museums and the Royal Palace.

To the right, the Rue de la Madeleine/Magdalena Steenweg leads along a small park to the **Chapel of St Mary Magdalene** (La Chapelle de la Madeleine/De Magdalenenkapel) **❶**, a Gothic prayer chapel dating from the 15th century, renovated in 1956. At that time the small baroque chapel of St Anna was moved here from the Rue de la Montagne/Bergstraat. The Rue de la Madeleine, continuing alongside the park, leads to **Albertinum Square** (Place de l'Albertine/Albertinaplein) **❷**, bordered by the Mont des Arts, the Palace of Congress and the huge complex of the Albertinum. This structure extends southeast where it is joined by the Museum of Older Art which in turn extends to the Rue de la Régence/Regentschapsstraat.

Statue in Albertinum Square

19

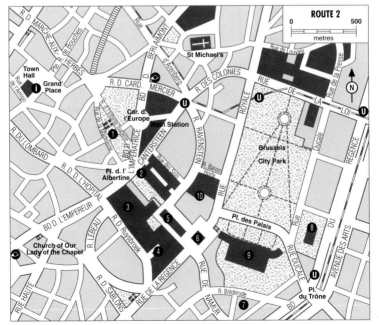

ROUTE 2
0   500
metres

Library of Albert I

Museum of Older Art

The Census of Bethlehem by Brueghel

The Albertinum, in its present form, was erected from 1954–65 as a memorial to King Albert I. It houses several libraries and museums. In the **Royal Library of Albert I** (Bibliothèque Royale Albert Ier/Koninklijke Bibliotheek Albert I) ❸ the working rooms of the poet Emile Verhaeren and the playwright Michael de Ghelderode have been reconstructed. The adjacent Book Museum (Musée du Livre/Museum van het Boek) houses an exhibition of the most important gifts to the library, valuable printed works and manuscripts, donated by the heirs of prominent families such as the Count de Launoit, the industrialist Solvay, the poet and artist Max Elskamp and the architect Henry van der Velde. The audio-visual department of the Museum of Sound (Musée de la Parole/Museum van de Stem) contains tape recordings of more than 5,000 famous voices.

The southeastern section (entrance on Rue de la Régence/Regentschapsstraat 3) houses the ★★ **Museum of Older Art** (Musée d'Art Ancien/Museum voor Oude Kunst) ❹. This was built in neoclassical style from 1875–81 based on plans by Balat. The four granite columns of the facade are crowned by bronze busts of Rubens, Jean Bologne and Jan van Ruijsbroek. To the side and above are two bronze groups, *The Crowning of the Fine Arts* (P de Vigne) and *The Inspiration of Art* (Van der Stappen). The museum's collection of paintings is mainly from the Flemish school of the 14th–17th century and includes works by such renowned artists as Brueghel the Elder, Rubens and Van Dyck, to name but a few. Additionally, the collection has constantly been expanded to include paintings up to and including the 19th-century.

The Royal Museum of Older Art was reopened in 1887 in the Palais Balat after originally being housed in the buildings of the former court of Charles of Lorraine. In the beginning, the collection was rather modest but it has grown so much over the course of time that more space, particularly for the works in the 19th-century department, is now necessary.

Massacre of the Innocents, Dirk Bouts

The Museum of Older Art contains works from the 14th, 15th and 16th centuries with an especially rare example of the painting of the pre-Van Eyck period, *Scenes from the Life of the Holy Virgin*, painted on wood and dating from the 14th century. Additionally, the museum houses three works of the Master of Flémalle including a *Prophecy*, six paintings by van der Weyden (1400-64) including the *Pietà* and the *Man with the Arrow*, two large paintings by Hugo van der Goes (1440-82), the two famous pictures of the four *Pictures of Righteousness* by Dirk Bouts (1415-75), paintings by Memling (1440-94), including *The Martyrdom of St Sebastian*, *The Holy Virgin with the Milk Soup* by Gerard David (1460-1523), *Crucifixion with Donor* and the triptych *The Temptation of St Anthony* by Hieronymus Bosch (1460-1516). The love that Pieter Brueghel the Elder (1520-69) had for his native landscapes is evidenced in a series of important paintings. The 16th-century department also contains numerous portraits as well as works by landscape artists (Patenier, Henri met de Bles, Bril, Van Coninxloo) and genre artists.

21

Another masterpiece by Brueghel, housed in the department of 16th–17th-century works, is part of the collection donated by Delporte. It is *A Winter Landscape with Ice Skaters and Bird Traps*. The Rubens Hall within the 17th-century department contains fabulous baroque creations by this master such as *The Assumption of the Virgin Mary*, *The Adoration of the Magi*, *The Martyrdom of St Livinus*, *Ascending Calvary* and the portrait of Hélène Fourment, the 16-year-old bride of Rubens.

The Jordaens Hall houses *The Allegory of Fertility* and, among the works of Van Dyck, the wonderful *Portrait of a Genoese Lady and Her Daughter*. Additionally, works by Fyt, Brouwer and Teniers as well as by 17th-century landscape artists hang here. This hall also contains works of the French, Dutch and Italian schools and several major works by Lucas Cranach the Elder.

The Rue de la Régence at this point crosses *Route 3*. Just a few hundred metres away is the church of Notre-Dame-des-Victoires-au-Sablon (*see page 27*). At the corner of Koningsplein/Place Royal is the entrance to the **Museum of Modern Art** (Musée d'Art Moderne/Museum voor Moderne Kunst) **5**. The eight floors of subterranean rooms, offering 1,200sq m (1,435sq yards) of exhibition space, are supplied with sufficient natural lighting via a

Gallery in the Museum of Modern Art

light shaft, which was added at the time of the museum's extensive renovation.

Of particular interest here are paintings, drawings and sculptures of the 19th- and 20th-century French and Belgian schools. The most important works of modern sculpture are in the large hall of the Museum of Modern Art. These include works by artists such as Constantin Meunier, E Souply, Rodin and César. The 19th-century paintings and the Paul Maas collection are representative of the Belgian and foreign schools: Classicism, Romanticism and Symbolism, Realism, Impressionism and Pointillism. The most important works of the collections are, in particular, those by the artists Alfred and Joseph Stevens and Louis Dubois (*Les Cigognes*). The museum also houses 29 paintings by Henri de Braekeleer including *Partie de cartes*, *Les Nèfles* and *La Femme du peuple*. Other famous works include *Temps de chien* and *Matinée pluvieuse à Ixelles* by G Vogels and *L'Art, les Caresses et le Sphinx* by Khnopff.

In the sculpture garden

The Belgian Impressionists exhibited here include Emil Claus, Anna Boch and I Verheyden. The French influence is evidenced in Theo van Rysselberghe's *Portrait of Madame Charles Maus*.

Several important works by French painters are also found here, including three paintings by Jean-Louis David (*La Mort de Marat*), the famous study *Apollon vainqueur du serpent python* by Delacroix, three Gauguin paintings and works by Courbet, Sisley, Signac, Corot and others. Other paintings of note hanging in the museum are Wouters' *Le Flûtiste*, Evenepoe's *Henriette au grand chapeau*, Permeke's *The Engaged Couple* and the Ostend native James Ensor's *Les Masques singuliers*. The Surrealists are represented by Paul Delvaux (*Pygmalion*) and René Magritte (*L'Empire des Lumières*). An entire room is devoted to Magritte. Additionally, masterpieces such as *Nu à contrejour* by Pierre Bonnard and *La Tentation de Saint Antoine* by Salvador Dalí are housed in this museum.

The **Place Royale**/Koningsplein **❻** was built in the 18th century by Barbané Guimard. Its classical architecture serves to glorify the reign of Charles of Lorraine. Numerous mansions line the square. The most important is that of Baron d'Arconati Visconti, later purchased by the family of the Counts of Flanders. Today it is the headquarters of a bank. In the middle of the square is a statue of Godfrey of Bouillon, the leader of the first crusade.

Across the Rue Montagne de la Court/Hofberg, which leads off the square to the northwest towards the Palace of Congress and Mont des Arts, is the church of Saint-Jacques-sur-Coudenberg. This towering structure, built in the classical style from 1776–85, has an impressive columned facade and a dome completed in 1845 (open

Godfrey of Bouillon statue in Place Royale

2–6pm). The route now leaves the Place Royale in a north-easterly direction towards the Place des Palais, located between the Royal Palace and the Brussels Park.

An alternative is to take a slight detour which leads around behind the palace complex, along the Rue de Namur/Naamsestraat, Rue Brederode/Brederodestraat, Place du Trône/Troonplein and Rue Ducale/Hertogstraat. This enables a stop at the **Dynasty Museum** (Musée de la Dynastie/Museum van de Dynastie) ❼ located at Rue Brederode 21. The museum houses a wealth of illustrated documents from the rulers of Belgium, dating from 1830 to the present. Also along this route, at the eastern end of the Palace Square, is the **Palace of the Academies** (Le Palais des Académies/Het Academienpaleis) ❽. Built in 1823–9 in Italian Renaissance style, it was designed as the residence of the Prince of Orange. In 1876 it was converted to the headquarters of the Belgian Royal Academy, founded by Maria Theresa in 1772.

Exhibit, Dynasty Museum

The **Royal Palace** (Palais du Roi/Koninklijk Paleis) ❾ was constructed under Leopold II, in the style of Louis XVI, during the second quarter of the 19th century. A copper statue of Leopold II (by Thomas Vincotte) is located behind the palace, which was built on the site of the former palace of the Duke of Brabant which burned down in 1731. That palace, known as the Brussels Court, was the residence of Philip the Good and Charles V. The new one, built by Van der Straeten, was renovated and expanded at the beginning of this century (1904–12). The sculptures in the gable are by Thomas Vincotte. The palace is open to visitors at certain times as the royal family no longer lives there. Their private residence is the Laeken Royal Palace *(see page 41)*.

Royal Palace

This tour continues on the other side of Rue Royale/Koningstraat, to the **Palace of Fine Arts** (Palais des Beaux-Arts/Paleis voor Schone Kunsten) ❿. This complex extends all the way to Rue Ravenstein, the location of the entrance. The Brussels Film Museum (Musée du Cinéma) is located at Rue Baron Horta/Baron Hortastraat No 9, the connecting street between Rue Royale and Rue Ravenstein. The museum shows old film classics daily. Baron Victor Horta, regarded as the originator of the art nouveau style, is the architect of the Palace of Fine Arts, built from 1921–8. It is still today, with its great halls for exhibitions, banquets and concerts, a focal point of Brussels' cultural life. Beside the palace, on Rue Ravenstein, is the Ravenstein House, the only remaining mansion in Brussels dating from the era of the Burgundian monarchy.

Ravenstein House

The return route to the Grand' Place leads over the Mont des Arts, across the Boulevard l'Empereur/Keizerslaan, along the Rue de l'Infante Isabella/Isabellastraat and past the Chapel of St Mary Magdalene again.

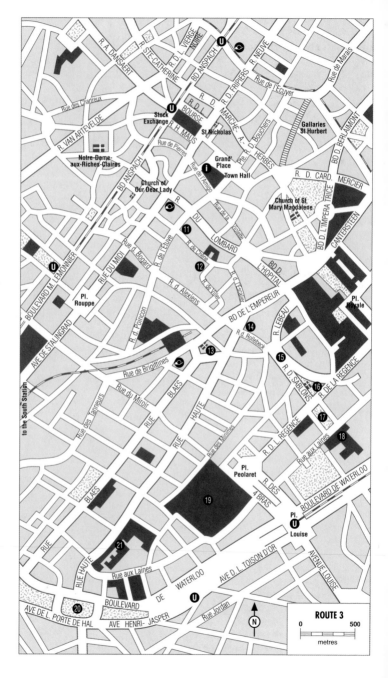

24

ROUTE 3

0   500

metres

N

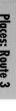

Route 3

Photographing the famous statue

★ Manneken Pis – ★ Church of Our Lady of the Chapel
(Notre-Dame-de-la-Chapelle) – Grand- and Petit-
Sablon Squares – Palace of Justice – ★ Porte de Hal –
Anneessens Tower

25

This route leaves the Grand' Place from beside the Town
Hall along the Rue Charles Buls/Karel Bulsstraat in a
southerly direction towards the Porte de Hal. Not far from
the Town Hall, at the corner of Rue de l'Etuve/Stoofstraat
(the continuation of Rue Charles Buls) and Rue du
Chêne/Eikstraat is the famous landmark of Brussels, the
★ **Manneken Pis ⓫**. This boy embodies the rebellious
spirit of the Brussels people. The small bronze statue was
created in the 17th century by the Belgian sculptor Jérôme
Duquesnoy.

The Manneken Pis

Many legends surround the figure. It is said that a citizen, whose run-away son had been restored to him,
promised to donate a statue depicting the boy looking as
perplexed as he did when he was found. Legend also has
it that after the theft of the statue by Louis XV's soldiers,
the king donated the costume of a marquis as an apol-
ogy. This became the first piece in the collection of the
Manneken Pis wardrobe now found in the Municipal Museum in the King's House (*see page 17*).

According to established rules of protocol, the figure
wears different uniforms to commemorate different events.
For example, on 6 April he wears a uniform of the American military police in honour of the day when the USA
entered World War I. On 30 April his garb is the uniform
of a French Legionnaire in memory of the French Foreign
Legion, and on 3 September the uniform of a guard from
the Welsh Guard Regiment in celebration of the liberation
of Brussels by this regiment in 1944. On 4 September

Our Lady of the Chapel

Manneken Pis wears the uniform of a soldier of the Piron Brigade. This is the anniversary of the day in 1914 when this brigade marched into Brussels. On 15 September he dons the uniform of an RAF pilot in memory of the Battle of Britain and on 27 October the uniform of a US sailor to celebrate Navy Day in America. On 20 November, when students at the University of Brussels honour their patron saint, Manneken Pis is dressed accordingly.

At the corner of Getrouwheidsgang/Rue de Fidélité (a street which comes to a dead end at Beenhouwersstraat) is Manneken's female counterpart, Jeanneken Pis. This bronze statue, 60cm (23 inches) tall, was created by the sculptor Lucie Genard.

The **Villers Tower** (Tour de Villers) **12**, located on Villerstraat/Rue de Villers, is a remnant of the former city wall dating from the 12th century.

One of the loveliest churches in Brussels is the **Church of Our Lady of the Chapel** (L'Eglise Notre-Dame-de-la-Chapelle/De Kapellekerk) **13**. The building provides evidence of several centuries of Brabant art and architecture. It was begun in the 12th century, but the nave seen today was mainly constructed in the 15th century, while the steeple dates from the early 18th century. Extensive restoration was carried out during the 19th century. The church is a harmonious union of a variety of architectural styles. A small Romanesque tower in the southern transept dates from the earliest epoch. Elements of early Gothic can also be found, while the steeple with its onion dome is in Renaissance style.

As early as the Middle Ages, the church was the centre of a working-class neighbourhood, today known as Les Marolles. The interior houses a carved wooden pulpit by Pierre Demis Plumier (early 18th-century), a 16th-century confessional, 17th century pillar sculptures and the tombs of Peter Brueghel the Elder and François Anneessens, an 18th-century guildsman executed for his part in a revolt.

The tour now leaves the Place de la Chapelle/Kapellenmarkt) along the Rue Haute/Hoogstraat behind the church and continues north (in the direction of the city centre), turning right at **Anneessens Tower** (La Tour d'Anneessens/Anneessenstoren) **14** into Rue de Rollebeek/Rollebeekstraat. This tower, also called Tour d'Angle/Hoektoren, is another remnant of the old city wall dating from the 12th century.

A centre for antique trading is **Grand-Sablon** (Place du Grand-Sablon/Grote Zavel) **15**. The Minerva Fountain in the centre of the square was a gift from Lord Bruce, Count of Ailesbury, in appreciation of the hospitality extended to him during his exile in Brussels. An antique and flea market is held here every weekend.

At the corner of the square and Petite Rue des Min-

Anneessens Tower

imes/Korte Miniemenstraat is the **Postal Museum** (Musée Postal) which documents the history of the postal system with a complete collection of Belgian as well as foreign stamps. It also houses a number of old and modern telecommunications devices. Between the Grand and Petite Sablon, on Rue de la Régence/Regentschapsstraat, is the **Church of Our Lady of the Victories** (Notre-Dame-des-Victoires-Au-Sablon/Zavelkerk) . It dates from the 15th–16th century and is recognised as one of the most superb examples of High-Gothic architecture in all of Belgium. The church, completely restored at the end of the 19th century, owes its magnificence to the archers of Brussels who were instrumental in its construction. Noteworthy in the interior: a gilt wooden chandelier, a candelabra dating from 1631, a carved wooden pulpit from 1697, the murals in the choir and a burial chapel of the family Thurn and Taxis. It was this family who initiated, from Brussels, the international postal service. The tombs of Count Lamoral (1678) and Garnier (1592), the secretary of the Duke of Parma, are also found in this church.

Rue de la Régence serves here as a link between Routes 2 and 3 (Museum of Older Art, *see page 20*).

Route 3 continues from the church across Rue de la Régence to the small park created in 1890 at **Petit-Sablon Square** (Place du Petit-Sablon/Kleine Zavel) ⓲. This was formerly a cemetery and is surrounded by an interesting wrought-iron fence. Small bronze statues, 48 in number, represent the craftsmen's guilds of the 16th century. In the middle of the gardens is a bronze group depicting the Counts of Egmont and Hoorn, the heroes of the Dutch resistance against the Spanish occupation in the 16th-cen-

Petit-Sablon Square

Church of Our Lady of the Victories

Egmont Palace

Peter Pan in the palace gardens

The Palace of Justice

tury, surrounded by renowned Humanists such as Mercator, Van Orley, Dodennée and others.

The Brussels Conservatory is at the corner of Rue de la Régence and the square (house No 17), in a building constructed by Cluysenaar in 1876–7. This structure is also home to the Museum of Musical Instruments (Musée Instrumental). Some parts of this collection of instruments, from all countries and epochs, many of which are unique, have recently been moved to house No 37 on Grand-Sablon Square. Behind Petit-Sablon Square, on Rue aux Laines/Wolstraat, stands the **Egmont Palace** (Palais d'Egmont/Egmontpaleis) ⓲ Originally constructed in the 16th century, it was acquired by the Arenberg family in the 18th century and renovated in Classical style. Today the palace is the residence of the Belgian Foreign Minister and is thus not open to the public. Its historic significance – Louis XV, Christine of Sweden and Voltaire resided here – was enhanced in 1972 when the Treaty of Accession to the European Community was signed here by Great Britain, Ireland and Denmark.

Adjacent to the palace is a park, parallel to Rue aux Laines (no access from this side). This leads to Poelaert Square and thus to one of the most conspicuous buildings in Brussels, the **Palace of Justice** (Palais de Justice/Justitiepaleis) ⓳ Construction was begun in 1866 by the architect Joseph Poelaert (1817-79) but was not completed until 1883, after his death. The dome towers 104m (333ft) above the city, making it visible far and wide.

With 25,000sq m (30,000sq yards), 27 assembly rooms and 245 smaller chambers, it is a monumental construction, probably the largest ever built in the 19th century.

Created in Graeco-Roman style, the building was erected on the site of the Brussels gallows. Its powerful form was designed to be reminiscent of the architecture of late antiquity as well as Egypt and Asia Minor. On both sides of the huge outdoor steps are colossal statues of Demosthenes, Lycurgus, Cicero and Ulpianus. Inside, the staircase of the entrance hall and the great hall crowned by the dome are architecturally of the greatest significance.

Palace of Justice entrance hall

Route 3 is the longest of the downtown walking tours described in this book. Those who wish to return to the starting point from here can walk around the Palace of Justice and follow Rue de Wynants/Wynantsstraat and Rue du Faucon/Valkstraat to Rue Haute/Hoogstraat, thus returning to the Grand' Place.

It is also possible to cross from Poelaert Square to the Place Louise/Louizaplein metro station, taking Line 2 to Arts Loi/Kunst Wet and changing there to Line 1 which leads to the main station near the Town Hall.

Those who wish to continue on this walk, however, can follow Route 3 to the southern tip of the city centre. From the Palace of Justice, walk along Rue aux Laines/Wolstraat to the end. Here, a short side street leads to a park between Boulevard de Waterloo/Waterloolaan and Avenue de la Porte de Hal/Hallepoortlaan. This is the site of one of the few remaining portions of the old city wall, dating from the year 1381 and restored in 1868–70, the gate called ★ **Porte de Hal** (Hallepoort) **20**. This is the only tower still standing from the second medieval city wall.

Porte de Hal Museum

From here, Rue Haute/Hoogstraat leads north and back into the city centre. On the right-hand side of the street, in the complex of the St Pierre Hospital (entrance at Rue Haute/Hoogstraat 298a) is the **Museum of Public Welfare** (Musée de l'Assistance Publique/Museum van de Openbare Onderstand) **21**. Paintings, sculptures and tapestries, goldsmiths' crafts and antique furniture from the most important charitable organisations of earlier ages, present a characteristic picture of the artistic milieu of Brussels and Brabant in the 15th to 18th century.

Exhibit in Porte de Hal

Rue Haute/Hoogstraat leads again past the Church of Our Lady of the Chapel and the Anneessens Tower (Tour d'Angle, *see page 26*) seen earlier on this tour. From here, one of two routes is possible. On the other side of the Boulevard de l'Empereur/Keizerslaan, either cross Dinant Square, passing the Manneken Pis again (the monument is quite small and might be overlooked) or continue more or less in a straight line along Rue de l'Escalier/Trapstrat, Place de la Vieille Halle-aux-Blés/Oude Korenhuis, Place Saint-Jean/St Jansplein and Rue de la Violette/Violetstraat to the Grand' Place. Although there are no sights of note along these streets, the route does provide an interesting peek behind the scenes of the Old Town.

Interior of Notre-Dame-du-Bon-Secours

Route 4

★ **Notre-Dame-du-Bon-Secours – Notre-Dame-aux-Riches-Claires – St Catherine's Square – Black Tower – Brouckère Square – Boulevard Anspach – Stock Exchange – St Nicholas Church**

This route also leaves the Grand' Place via Rue Charles Buls/Karel Buisstraat and its extension, Rue de l'Etuve/Stoofstraat. At the Manneken Pis (*see page 25*), however, it turns right into Rue des Grands Carmes/Lievevrouwbroersstraat. At the end of this street, after the intersection with the main street Rue du Midi/Zuidstraat, is the ★ **Church of Notre-Dame-du-Bon-Secours** (Onze-Lieve-Vrouw van Bijstand-Kerk) ㉒. It is built in the Flemish Renaissance style of the 17th century and contains a statue of the Holy Virgin which is reputed to have miraculous powers.

Statue of the Holy Virgin

The church is at the corner of Rue du Marché-au-Charbon/Kolenmarkt and Rue du Jardin des Olives/Olivetenhof. The latter street ends, after just a few metres, at the expansive Boulevard Anspach/Anspachlaan. For those interested in a short tour, follow this boulevard north to the Stock Exchange (*see page 32*). To see other sights in the western part of the city centre, however, cross the main street and take the next left. This boulevard, by the way, divides the Brussels Old Town into the Lower City to the west and the Upper City to the east.

Rue des Riches-Claires/Rijkelarenstraat leads to the church of **Notre-Dame-aux-Riches-Claires**/Rijkelarenkerk ㉓. Its gables depict a typical Brussels conception

of Italian Renaissance. It is the work of Luc Fayd'herbe (1617–97), a pupil of Rubens known above all for his creation of colossal statues adorning the pillars of the church nave. A bit further west, Rue Saint-Christophe/Sint-Kristoffelstraat branches off to the right. This leads to Rue du Vieux Marché-aux-Grains/Oude Graanmarkt which continues on to **St Catherine's Square** (Place Ste-Catherine/Sint-Katelijneplein)  with the church of the same name, dating from the 14th–15th century. This church, in a very poor state of repair, was reconstructed in a mixture of Romanesque and Renaissance style in 1854–5 by Joseph Poelaert, the architect of the Palace of Justice. The 17th-century **St Catherine's Tower** (Tour Ste-Catherine/Sint-Katelijnetoren) is the only remaining part of this church's predecessor. In the left-hand aisle stands the Black Madonna, dating from the 14th–15th century. The statue was originally carved from light-coloured stone, but over the years it has become almost completely blackened.

St Catherine's Church

The **Black Tower** (Tour Noire/Zwarte Toren) is one of the rare remains of the first city wall from the 12th century. It was restored in 1888–9. Crossing over Samedi Square and following along Rue du Cyprès/Cipressstraat, the route leads to the **Beguine Church** (St-Jean-Baptiste-au-Béguinage/Begijnhofkerk van Sint-Jan) , a masterpiece of 17th-century baroque architecture.

The Black Tower

Originally the church was a Gothic basilica. It was renovated in 1657–76, at which time the present-day facade, a splendid example of the Flemish exuberance of Belgian baroque architecture, was created. The 18th-century high altar as well as paintings from the Rubens school, including works by Van Loon, De Crayer and Otto Venius (*Entombment*) adorn the interior. The Beguine community itself, which totalled 1,200 members in its heyday, was dissolved during the 19th century.

After passing this series of monumental structures in the western part of the city centre, the tour now leads along Rue de Laeken/Laekenstraat and Rue des Hirondelles/Zwaluwenstraat directly to the centre of the business and entertainment area of Brussels, **Brouckère Square** (Place de Brouckère/De Brouckèreplein) 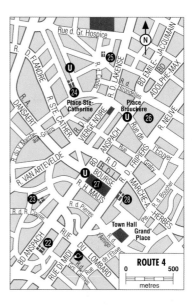. It is here that the city's two main streets, Boulevard Anspach leading from the south and Boulevard Adolphe-Max (*see Route 5, page 33*) from the north, merge. In the 1970s, the new metro Line 3 was constructed under these two thoroughfares as well as under Boulevard Maurice-Lemonnier leading south. This reduced at least somewhat the traffic chaos along this north–south axis through the downtown area by eliminating the public transportation vehicles from the streets. This underground link between the North and South stations crosses the east–west metro line (Line 1) at the southern end of Place de Brouckère. Line 1 leads east to the Europe Centre (*see page 44*).

A visit to this square and the surrounding area after sunset, when the colourful lights of the commercial establishments twinkle on, can be highly recommended.

The fountain at the church of St Catherine's, not far from Brouckère Square, was created in 1897 by F Janlet and originally stood on this square. By now this route has probably turned into a shopping spree along Boulevard Anspach which leads south from Brouckère Square past the Centre Monnaie/Muntcentrum with its large, modern shopping arcade.

The Stock Exchange

Before returning to the Grand' Place, the route leads past two more interesting buildings. One, located at the Place de la Bourse (Beursplein), a square located directly on Boulevard Anspach, is the **Stock Exchange** (La Bourse/De Beurs) **27**, the centre of Brussels' financial life. This institution changed location several times after its original foundation in the former Augustinian Monastery in 1801, but the present massive edifice was only conceived when the city councillors became aware of its importance for the city. It was constructed in 1868–75 by Léon Suys the Younger in neo-baroque style. The triangular tympanum is supported by Corinthian columns and a relief by J Jacquet depicts Belgium's defence through commerce and industry.

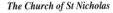

The Church of St Nicholas

Diagonally across from the rear facade, at the end of Rue de la Bourse/Beurstraat, is the **Church of St Nicholas** (L'Eglise Saint-Nicolas/Sint-Niklaaskerk) **28**, dedicated to the patron saint of the merchants. As one of the oldest churches, its historical development is similar to that of the city. It has been repeatedly renovated over the course of time and in 1955 received a totally new facade. The interior of the church is richly decorated with works of art: the altar in the left aisle is adorned with a 15th-century Madonna; the pillar on the right-hand side of the choir supports a Spanish figure of Christ dating from the 16th century; the painting of the *Virgin and Child Asleep* is attributed to Rubens.

A copper shrine in front of the pulpit recalls the Masters of Gorcum, who were put to death in Brielle (near Rotterdam) after suffering unspeakable torture at the hands of the Gueux.

From here, along Rue au Beurre/Boterstraat, it is only a short way back to the starting point of this route, the Town Hall on the Grand' Place.

Route 5

**Finistère Church – Boulevard Ring – North Station
– Botanical Garden – Martyrdom Square – Théâtre
Royal de la Monnaie**

This route, leading through the northern sector of the city
centre, leaves the Grand' Place to the left of the King's
House via the tiny Rue Chair et Pain/Vlees-en-Broodstraat,
Meat and Bread Street. Shortly thereafter it turns left into
Rue du Marché-Aux-Herbes/Grasmarkt. This, and the ad-
joining Rue du Marché-aux-Poulets/Kiekenmarkt, lead

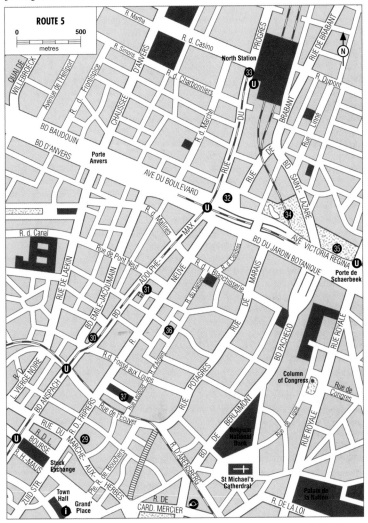

Finistère Church

The boulevard ring

Botanical Garden

directly to the expansive Boulevard Anspach/Anspach-laan. It is also possible to take the first street to the right, Rue de la Fourche/Greepstraat, walking through the arcades of Galerie Du Centre ㉙ and Galerie St-Honoré, before arriving at Rue du Marché-aux-Poulets. This leads to Boulevard Anspach and Place de Brouckère ㉚, which are described in *Route 4 (see page 30)*, where the route turns right, towards the north.

Along Boulevard Adolphe-Max, a wide shopping avenue heading north from Brouckère Square, is, at the corner of a tiny street of the same name, the **Finistère church** (L'Eglise au Finistère/Finesterraekerk) ㉛. It was built in 1708 and contains a Gothic statue of Mary which comes from Aberdeen, called *Notre-Dame-du-Bon-Succès* (*Onze Lieve Vrouw van Goed Geluk*).

As a shortcut, it is possible to continue along Finistère Street to Rue aux Choux/Koolstraat, completing the ring (*see below*). The other alternative is to follow Boulevard Adolphe-Max further north to Place Charles Rogier ㉜, a major traffic junction. This is the intersection of the north–south boulevard, which links the North Station (Gare du Nord/Noordstation) with the South Station (Gare du Midi/Zuidstation), and the expansive boulevard ring, a motorway around the city centre.

The wide **boulevard ring** was constructed along the lines of the old city wall which until that time had encircled the Old Town. The motorway, with a length of 7km (4 miles), was built in the middle of the 19th century. It has been modernised since then and is now free of crossings, running through tunnels and over bridges. The ring is the major motor route within the city; without it Brussels, with the amount of traffic passing through it today, would be chaotic. In recent times two metro lines have also been constructed beneath Charles Rogier Square. Metro line 2 leads under the boulevard ring in a clockwise direction and currently has seven stations. Metro line 3 directly links the North and South stations.

About 500m north of Charles Rogier Square on Rue du Progrès/Vooruitgangsstraat, outside of the ring, is the North Station with its **Railway Museum** (Musée du Chemin de Fer/Spoorwegmuseum) ㉝. Of great interest to railway enthusiasts, it contains historical documents, models (including locomotives), uniforms and other material depicting the development of the Belgian railway system. The entrance is at Rue du Progrès 76.

Also on the other side of the ring, bearing the appropriate name Boulevard du Jardin Botanique/Kruidtuin-laan, is the **Botanical Garden** (Jardin Botanique National de Belgique/Nationale Plantentuin van Belgie) ㉞. These public gardens extend eastward from the original site and form Belgium's most important collection of exotic trees and plants. The original gardens, laid out along the ring in 1826–30 according to plans by Gineste, became state property in 1870. The greenhouse  at the corner of Rue Royale/Koningsstraat and Rue Botanique/Kruidtuinstraat was built in 1826 by T F Suys. It is constructed of iron and glass with rows of ionic pillars. Because city planners realised that a further expansion on this site was not possible, a new botanical garden was created in 1944 in the Domäne Bouchout north of Brussels (*see page 42*).

Martyrdom Square

The return route leads parallel to Boulevard Adolphe-Max, along Rue des Centres/Asstraat, Rue du Damier/Dambordstraat and Rue des Oeillets/Anjelierenstraat, and on to **Martyrdom Square** (Place des Martyrs/Martelaarsplein **36**. The architect Claude Antoine Fisco designed this square in the austere beauty of the neoclassical style. Recent renovations were completed in 1994. The 450 heroes who gave their lives fighting the Dutch in the revolution of 1830 are buried in the crypt underneath the monument, *Belgia*, which stands in the centre of the square. Designed by G Geefs, it was consecrated on 4 October 1830 in the presence of government officials, the army and numerous Belgian patriots.

35

Théâtre Royal de la Monnaie

The Brussels opera house, the **Théâtre Royal de la Monnaie** (Muntschouwburg) **37**, gets its name from the national mint that originally stood on this site and minted the coins for the Duchy of Brabant. This theatre, the site of many opera premières, has a reputation as one of the finest opera houses in the world. It was also the scene of one of the most important historic events in the city, for it was here, on the night of 25 August 1830, that the revolution which was to lead to the country's independence was actually triggered.

The opera Masianello (also known as La Muette de Portici), by Daniel François Esprit Auber and based on the Neapolitan Revolution of 1647, had been scheduled for performance at the opera house, but, following unrest in the city, the authorities had felt it wise to postpone its run. The première was finally held on 25 August before a packed house. Its effect on the audience was electrifying. As the opera progressed they became increasingly agitated, and when, in Act IV, the call to arms rang out, it could not be contained. With patriotic cries on their lips they streamed out of the auditorium towards the houses occupied by Dutch families, and then to the municipal park. The revolution had begun.

To return to the Grand' Place two routes are possible. The first is along Rue de l'Ecuyer/Schildknaapstraat, Rue des Dominicains/Predikherenstraat and Petite Rue de Bouchers/Korte Beenhouwersstraat. The alternative is to continue along Rue de l'Ecuyer and return via the famous Galerie Saint-Hubert.

Route 6

Galeries Saint-Hubert – ★ St Michael's Cathedral – Column of Congress – Parliament Building – Brussels Park – Royal Palace

The last route through the city centre leaves the Grand' Place via Rue de la Colline/Heuvelstraat, the same path as *Route 2 (see page 19)*, and leads to the eastern part of the downtown area. The two routes join at the southern end of Brussels Park, in front of the Royal Palace *(see page 23)* thus making it possible to combine both routes into one longer tour.

At the end of Rue de la Colline, on the other side of Rue du Marché aux Herbes/Grasmarkt, are the **Galeries Saint-Hubert** (Sint-Hubertus-Galerijen) **㉟**, built in 1846 as the first glass-covered shopping arcade in Europe. The main gallery has a length of 200m (656ft). Rue des Bouchers/Beenhouwersstraat cuts through it, roughly in the middle, dividing the arcade into the Galerie de la Reine/

Galeries Saint-Hubert

36

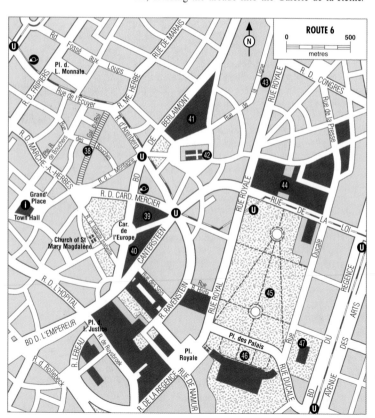

Inside the galleries

Koninginnegalerij (Queen's Gallery) and the Galerie du Roi/Koningsgalerij (King's Gallery). A third section, branching off to the left from the latter is known as the Gallery of Princes. This extends to Rue des Dominicains/Predikherenstraat.

37

At the end of the main gallery the route turns left into Rue d'Arenberg/Arenbergstraat which leads to Boulevard de l'Impératrice/Keizerinlaan. To the right, on this boulevard, is Sabena House **39**. It houses the Air Terminal and the main station of Brussels (Gare Centrale/Centraal Station) **40**, first opened in 1952 upon completion of the six-track subterranean railway station linking the North and South stations. To the left is the huge Belgian National Bank complex **41**, which was built in 1860 and expanded in 1905. In 1951, a new facade was added, creating the impressive building seen here today.

The next sight is the powerful Gothic structure of Brussels' principal place of worship. Its complete name is the Church of St Michael and St Gudula (Collégiale Saint-Michel et Sainte-Gudule), but it is more usually referred to simply as ★ **St Michael's Cathedral** (Cathédrale Saint-Michel/ Sint-Michiels Kathedraal) **42**. The nave and aisles, after renovations carried out over several years, have now been restored to their original beauty. The impressive structure was built in 1226 when it became apparent that the existing Romanesque church was too small. The main elements of its facade are vertical, making it more reminiscent of German Gothic than of the French architecture of this period. The choir, transept and southern aisle date from the 13th century while the northern aisle, nave and both of the unfinished 69-m (226-ft) high towers are from the 14th–15th century. The side chapel, housing the tombs of the Dukes of Brabant, was added between the 16th–17th century.

St Michael's Cathedral

Stained glass in St Michael's

The stained-glass windows in the choir, the transept and

some of the chapels are especially beautiful. Many of these magnificent windows were created from drawings by Van Orley and were a gift from Charles V and his family. The carved pulpit from 1699 and the Brussels tapestries woven by Van der Borght in 1785 (displayed only on religious holidays) are of particular note.

Restoration work

The church was restored in the 19th century at which time the huge outdoor steps were added. Other sights in the interior of the church include:

In the nave: statues of the apostles on the pillars, carved by Jérôme Duquesnoy the Younger (Paul, Matthew, Bartholomew, Thomas), by Luc Faid'herbe (Simon), by Jan van Milder (Philip, Andrew) and by Tobias de Lelis (Peter, John); the above-mentioned pulpit by Henri F Verbruggen (1699) depicting the banishment from Paradise; the animals, at the steps, by Van der Haeghen (1780); and the 16th-century stained-glass window of the portal portraying *The Last Judgment* by J de Vriendt.

In the transept: stained-glass windows by Barend van Orley depicting Charles V, Isabella of Portugal and Louis the Great of Hungary with his wife Maria as well as paintings by M Coxie (*Crucifixion and Entombment, The Life of St Gudula*).

In the choir: the late 16th-century stained-glass windows above the high altar, depicting from left to right Maximilian of Austria and Mary of Burgundy, Philip the Fair and Joanna of Castile, Charles V and his brother Ferdinand, Philip II and Mary of Portugal, Philibert of Savoy and Margaret of Austria. Behind the high altar is the tomb of Duke John II of Brabant, who died in 1312, and his wife. Across from this is the tomb of Archduke Ernst (died 1595) with the statue by Robert de Nole.

In the Chapel of the Virgin (de la Vierge): stained-glass windows by Jean de la Baer (1656–63) based on drawings by van Thulden as well as portraits of the donor Emperor Ferdinand III and his wife Eleonore, Emperor Leopold I, Archduke Albrecht and Isabella, Archduke Leopold Wilhelm.

In the Chapel of the Miracle of the Holy Sacrament (du Saint-Sacrement de Miracle): stained-glass windows depicting the miracle of the sacrament. According to biblical legend, the stolen Host began to flower, thus leading to the discovery of the culprit who was burned alive as punishment.

In the lower part of the window are portraits of the donors Catherine and John III of Portugal, Louis of Hungary and Maria, King Francis I of France and Eleonore as well as Ferdinand I and Anna of Poland. The stained-glass windows were executed from 1542–7 according to drawings by M Coxie and Barend van Orley.

Behind the church and the National Bank, beginning at

the corner of Rue de la Banque/Bankstraat and Rue des Bois-Sauvage/Wildewouldstraat, is Rue de la Ligne/De Lignestraat which leads to the 47-m (154-ft) high **Column of Congress** (Colonne du Congrès/Kongreszuil) ❹ in Congress Square. It was built in 1850–9 according to plans by Joseph Poelaert. It commemorates the National Congress which created the Belgian constitution after the declaration of independence in 1830. The platform at the top of the column is now closed to the public for reasons of safety. The Brussels Administrative Centre (Cité Administrative/Administrative Wijk) is adjacent to the northern end of this square.

Column of Congress

From this northernmost point of the walking tour, the path leads south along Rue Royale/Koningsstraat, continuing to the corner of Rue de la Loi/Wetstraat where the **Parliament Building** (Palais de la Nation/Palais der Natie) ❹ is located. Both houses of the Belgian parliament, the House of Representatives and the Senate, convene here. Visitors can watch a video tape tour of the building or can observe a parliamentary session from the gallery. The offices of various ministries are housed in the part of the palace adjacent to the parliament sector.

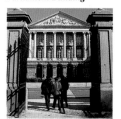
Parliament Building

39

In former times, the complex was the seat of the Advisory Council of the Duchy of Brabant. The structure was originally built from 1779–83 by Guimard. It was rebuilt about 100 years later (1884–7) after having been destroyed by fire. From here, Rue de la Loi leads east across the boulevard ring to the European Community Headquarters (Communauté Européene/Europese Gemeenschappen). A bit further on is Cinquantenaire Park and Palace with a number of important museums. All of these sights are described in Route 8 (*see page 44*).

The classical facade of the Palais de la Nation looks out over a square of the same name. Beyond the square is **Brussels Park** (Parc de Bruxelles/Park van Brussel or De Warande) ❹, the former hunting grounds of the dukes of Brabant. It was converted in 1776 to French gardens by the Austrian Anton Zinner. Today this fenced-in tract, 13ha (32 acres) in size, is the largest park in the city centre. Its paths are lined with numerous statues. The only building within the park is the Royal Park Theatre (Théâtre Royal du Parc/Koninklijk Parktheater), located in the northeast corner. The entrance is on Rue de la Loi.

Relaxing in Brussels Park

At the southern end of the park is the **Royal Palace** ❹ while the **Palace of the Academies** ❹ is located along the southeastern side. Both of these structures are described in greater detail in Route 2 (*see page 23*). To return to the starting point from here, follow Route 2 in either direction. This gives you the alternative of returning directly to the Grand' Place or of returning via Place Royale and Mont des Arts.

A statue by the path

Route 7

Brussels Harbour – Laeken – Royal Palace – Domäne Bouchout (Botanical Garden) – Grimbergen Abbey – Convention Centre – ★★ Atomium

Brussels Harbour

Almost all of the main streets exiting the northern part of the boulevard ring between Place Sainctelette/Saincteletteplein in the northwest and Porte de Schaerbeek/Schaarbeesepoort in the northeast lead to the park-like northern sector of Brussels. These streets all feed into Avenue de la Reine/Koninginnelaan which crosses the Sea Canal immediately north of **Brussels Harbour** and leads to the large park grounds of Laeken. First, however, a few words about the harbour, located between Avenue du Port/Havenlaan and Allée Verte/Groenlaan.

As early as 1434, as the Senne became increasingly silted, Brussels was given permission by Duke Philip the Good to dredge a channel in the river. But this measure proved unsatisfactory and in 1477 Mary of Burgundy granted permission to dig a canal alongside the river. It was designed to link the Senne to the Rupel at Willebroek. It was completed in 1561 and shortly thereafter three harbour basins were constructed in Brussels. The canal was first deepened in 1819–36. Two phases of expansion, beginning in 1902, eventually converted the Willebroek into a sea canal. A sea harbour, with all of the necessary technical facilities, was also constructed at that time. In 1922 the canal was finally opened to ocean-going vessels with a draught of up to 5.8m (19ft). The Brussels port was then linked to the southern Belgian industrial

Traffic on the canal

region via the Charleroi Canal and, via the Willebroek Canal, to the Scheldt and thus right to the open sea.

On the other side of the canal, Avenue de la Reine leads into Avenue du Parc Royal/Koninklijk Parklaan. Here, on the left, is the **Church of Notre-Dame-de-Laeken** (Onze-Lieve-Vrouwkerk van Laeken) 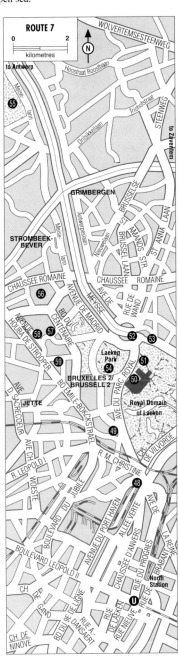, a good 4km (2½ miles) from the Grand' Place. It was constructed from 1854–72 by Poelaert in memory of Louise-Maria, the first queen of Belgium. A miraculous Virgin, dating from the 13th century, attracts many worshippers. Aside from the royal crypt, this church also contains the tombs of many prominent personalities including, among others, Poelaert and Suys.

Park Avenue continues north from the church through several curves. The former royal domain of Laeken (Domaine Royale/Koninklijk Domein), is on the right. This is the location of the huge **Royal Palace** (Palais du Roi/Koninklijk Paleis) **50**. The palace, still the residence of the royal family, is closed to the public. It was built by Montoyer in the second half of the 18th century and later renovated under Leopold II in Louis XVI style. It was expanded by Girault in 1903. Napoleon, a frequent resident of the palace, signed the declaration of war against Russia here. The main attraction is the series of 11 connected art nouveau greenhouses **51** built in Leo-pold II's reign between 1876–95.

The most magnificent part of this exotic world of plants is the winter garden. The greenhouses are only open to the public for a few days in April and May. The opening times are announced in the newspapers and on the radio. The tourist office *(see page 96)* will also have this information.

Just a short distance from the greenhouses is the **Neptune Fountain** (Fontaine de Neptune/Neptunusfontein) **52**, a replica of the splendid fountain created by the sculptor Jean de Bologne in 1566 for Piazza del Nuttuno in Bologna. Nearby, skirted today by the busy north–south motorway linking Brussels with Antwerp, is the **Chinese Pavilion** (Pavillon Chinois/Chinees Pavilioen) **53**. Leopold II purchased the structure at the Paris World Exhibition in 1900

41

Chinese Pavilion

and had it placed on this spot in 1910. It originally served as a restaurant, but today it houses a priceless collection of 17th- and 18th-century Chinese porcelain.

Across from the Royal Palace, on the west side of Park Avenue, is the Laeken Public Park (Parc de Laeken/Laekenpark), site of the **Belvédère Palace 54** which was built for Viscount de Walckiers in 1788 and is today the residence of the Prince of Liège. In the middle of the central traffic circle (Place de la Dynastie/Vorstenhuisplein) is a monument to Leopold I.

Botanical Garden

At this point a decision must be made as to whether to take a detour to the new location of the Brussels Botanical Garden (*see page 34*) in **Domäne Bouchout 55** (*see Map of surrounding area, page 9*). If you choose to visit the garden, drive onto the Antwerp motorway at the northern end of Park Avenue and take the exit for Strombeek-Bever. The next exit, Meise, is beyond Bouchout. The royal domain is located at the southern end of the town of Meise. The Botanical Garden, which now extends to 93ha (230 acres) was moved here in 1944 from its former location on the ring near the North Station.

The huge new greenhouse in Domäne Bouchout measures 155 x 78 x 19m (509 x 256 x 62ft). The arrangement of the plants takes into account their geographical origins while also relying on principles of landscaping.

The Herbarium, a part of the Botanical Garden, contains various scientific collections of plants as well as a special library of botany. Whereas the greenhouses are open to the public, use of the Herbarium is limited to scientists and researchers.

In the middle of the park is a 12th-century moated castle, renovated in the 17th century and again in the 19th, when it acquired its neo-Gothic style. It served as the occasional residence of Empress Charlotte.

St Servais Church

The **Grimbergen Abbey**, only 7km (4 miles) from Meise, is situated directly on the road between Meise and Vilvoorde. Noteworthy in the unique baroque church of St Servais are the confessional, pulpit and choir pews as well as a ceiling fresco in the vestry. From here, it is possible to return to Brussels via Vilvoorde, but if you decide on this route you will miss the following sights.

In the Heysel section of town is the International Conference Centre (Centre International de Conférences/International Conferentiecentrum) with the **Centenaire Halls** (Palais du Centenaire/Eeuwfeestpaleizen) **56**. These halls, which also serve as the site of the Brussels International Sample Trade Fair, were originally constructed in 1935 and then expanded for the World Exhibition of 1958. The name derives from the centennial of Belgian independence. The complex of buildings is one of the largest exhibition and trade fair centres in Europe.

At the end of Boulevard du Centenaire/Eeuwfeestlaan, which leads from the exhibition halls back towards the city, is the ★★ **Atomium** ❺❼. This bizarre-looking structure was designed for the 1958 World Exhibition, to symbolise the potential of Belgian industry at the time. With a height of 102m (335ft), it is based on the fundamental concept of an iron molecule, enlarged to 165 billion times its original size. The nine atoms are depicted by nine hollow steel spheres, each with a diameter of 18m (59ft). After the exhibition, the City of Brussels placed a formal request that its new landmark should not be dismantled. A permanent exhibit called Pioneering in Medicine examines the developments which have taken place in the fields of virology, immunology and genetics.

The Atomium

An express lift in the central connecting strut takes you to the restaurant in the highest of the nine spheres. The numerous windows provide a breathtaking panorama of the city. After dark, points of light skip from one sphere to the next, symbolising the path of the electrons around the atomic nucleus.

The **Brussels Planetarium** ❺❽ is located on Avenue de Bouchout/Boechoutlaan which leads westwards from the Atomium. The Heysel sports stadium ❺❾ is also located on this street.

43

Another sight near the Atomium is the gigantic amusement park, **Brupark**. Replicas of historical and modern structures, representing the 12 countries of the European Economic Community, have been built here on a scale of 1:25, resulting in a kind of mini Europe. The tropical swimming pool and the cinema complex with 14 theatres are popular with tourists and residents alike.

Brupark Amusement Park

Route 8

East and southeast of the city centre: Route 8A: Europe Centre – Cinquantenaire Park – Cinquantenaire Arch – Army Museum – ★ Museum of Art and History. Route 8B: Woluwe-St Pierre – Val Duchesse Abbey – Museum of Central Africa in Tervuren

The distance from the centre of the city to the various sights in the east and southeast sections of Brussels varies greatly. The Europe Centre and Cinquantenaire Park are only about 2km (1.2 miles) from the Parliament Building (*see page 39*) and can thus be reached by foot along Rue de la Loi/Wetstraat, crossing over the eastern section of the ring.

Val Duchesse Abbey

Val Duchesse Abbey, on the other hand, is about 7km (4 miles) away and the Museum of Central Africa is 14km (8 miles) from the centre.

Route 8A takes you to the sights which are closer to the centre. If you are travelling by car you can continue on to the outskirts of the city, thus reaching Route 8B.

Route 8A

At the eastern end of Rue de la Loi/Wetstraat, surrounding Rond Point Robert Schuman/R Schumanplein is the **Europe Centre**, the Administrative Headquarters of the European Community (Communauté Européenne/Europese Gemeenschappen) **60**. The main building north of the square, with its four wings, is especially prominent. This structure, which houses over 100 international organisations, will soon be torn down because of its high asbestos content. Nearby are the railway station and the metro stations for Lines 1A and 1B which lead downtown from the Europe Centre and Cinquantenaire Park to Place de Brouckère and the central station. These stations are all named after the founder of the EC, Robert Schuman.

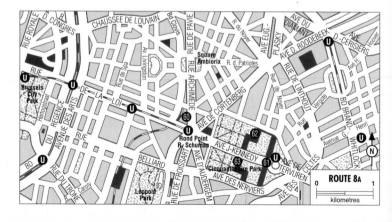

Cinquantenaire Arch

Avenue Kennedy begins to the east of Schuman Square, leading through **Cinquantenaire Park** (Parc du Cinquantenaire/Jubelpark) to the **Cinquantenaire Arch** (Arcade du Cinquantenaire/Triomfboog van het Jubelpark) **61**. The park and palace were built under Leopold II in honour both of the 50th anniversary of Belgium's independence (thus the French name Cinquantenaire) and of the 1897 World Exhibition held at the eastern edge of the Quartier Léopold. There are several monuments in the park including a Congo memorial and an African memorial, both by Thomas Vincotte. A small temple-like structure houses a marble relief entitled *Human Passions* by J Lambeaux.

The triumphal arch, visible from afar, is 60m (197ft) wide and 45m (148ft high). It was constructed according to plans by Girault and links the two wings of the **Cinquantenaire Palace**. The Quadriga over the arch is the work of Vincotte and Lagae. Figures from the Belgian provinces are seen on the column pedestals. The Cinquantenaire Palace, built by Bordiau for the Brussels World Exhibition in 1897, today houses the **Royal Museum of Army and Military History** (Musée Royale de l'Armée et d'Histoire Militaire/Koninklijk Museum van het Legeren Militaire Geschiedenis) **62** in its north wing. The collections include military relics from the late 18th century and thereafter, but mainly from World War I. The historical section contains a variety of pieces relating to battles which took place on Belgian soil.

Exhibit in the military museum

Military aircraft on display

The museum also has a library with 70,000 volumes about war history and war technology as well as documents, photographic collections, prints and maps. In the south wing, which was later renovated and expanded (entrance at Avenue des Nerviers/Nervierslaan) is the ★ **Royal Museum of Art and History** (Musée d'Art et d'Histoire/De Koninklijke Museum voor Kunst en Geschiedenis) **63**. These collections were founded in 1880 (as were the park and palace) and, until 1929, the building was

45

Museum of Art and History
A mosaic display

known as the Cinquantenaire Museum. The collections are divided into the following departments: Antiquities, Decorative Arts (Industrial Arts), Ancient Belgium and General Archaeology, Folk Art and Ethnology. A portion of the south wing which was part of the Department of Antiquities burned down in 1946. Fortunately, almost all the objects of value were saved from the flames. The museum also has a specialist library which contains classical scientific works. A special feature of the museum is that blind visitors can examine the exhibits by touch.

The following are a few examples from the wealth of exhibits in the main departments of the museum:

Belgian Collections

From prehistoric times: utensils, models of three stages of human development (Neanderthal, Crô-Magnon, Neolithic), models of grottoes in which prehistoric finds were made, the archaeological sites and finds from Bruyère and Baelen, vases, weapons, tombs, tools of polished stone, bronze weapons and tools, archaeological maps of Belgian territory from different eras.

From the Iron Age: weapons, tools, urns and vases, plus early coins.

From the Roman Age in Belgium: wooden wells, brick and other construction materials, vases, bronzeware, glass and rock crystal objects, tombstones.

From the Frankish Era: weapons, models of living quarters and graves, clasps, jewellery, combs, coins and glassware.

Oriental Collections

From Asia Minor: cast of the obelisk of Salmanassar III, various objects of Sumerian and Babylonian origin, cuneiform texts from Babylonia and Assyria dating from the fourth millenium to the second century BC, casts of Assyrian statues and reliefs, a fine collection of pottery cylinders and bricks.

From Upper Egypt (Prehistoric Age): collection of pottery, weapons and stone vases, jewellery, cosmetic objects, an Egyptian tomb whose walls are covered with reliefs and inscriptions.

From Egypt (Old Kingdom): objects from the tombs of the first dynasties, pottery, jewellery, parts of reliefs and statues as well as tombs from the sixth dynasty.

From Egypt (Middle Kingdom and New Kingdom): stone and wood coffins, painted statuettes, vases of clay and stone, jewellery, seals, scarabs, fragments of reliefs from the Temple of Deir el Báhari, bronze items, enamelled pottery as well as wooden and granite statuettes.

Egypt (Middle Kingdom)

47

From Egypt (New Kingdom): painted pottery vases, part of an obelisk, part of a statue of the wife of King Ramses II, statue of the God Khonsou (21st dynasty), enamelled and faience pottery, amulets, wooden coffins (mostly from Deir el Báhari), parts of a book of the dead and a reconstruction of the tomb of Nakht.

From Egypt (Saitic Era): statuettes from tombs, part of a stone sculpture, mummies and coffins, bronze statuettes of gods and animals, stone vases, pottery and glass, tools and articles of clothing.

From Egypt (Greek-Roman Era): mummies and coffins. Also antiquities from Nubia and Sudan.

Greek and Roman Collections

Greek vases from the 5th century BC, vases and vessels from the neolithic and Mycenaean period, vases in geometric style, Etruscan, Ionian and Corinthian vases, red vases with black figures, vessels from Mycenaea (gold, 1500BC), black vases with red figures; 5th- and 6th-century sculptures, sculptures from Greek and Roman times; colossal bronze statue of Septimius Severus, Roman sarcophagus; frescoes from Bosco Reale, lead sarcophagus and bronze works ; glasses, combs, jewellery, small bronze trinkets, mirrors; terra-cotta and Tanagra figures; Phoenician, Hellenistic, Carthaginian and Roman antiquities; casts which show the development of Greek and Roman sculpture.

Greek Sculpture

Decorative Arts

Gothic: Gothic cradle from 1480, 15th-century wood carvings, tapestries from Tournai (15th-century, *Battle of Roncevaux*, *Legend of Hercules*); early 16th-century Brussels tapestries; 15th-century coverlet, Madonna, proclamation from the 15th century (marble, French school of 14th century), tapestry from Tournai (early-16th century, *Sheep Shearing*), tapestries from Brussels (first half of 16th cen-

tury; *Mary with the Christ Child and St Anne and St Luke*):
15th-century furniture.

Renaissance: Christ on the cross (wood, southern
Netherlands, 16th-century); carved and painted wooden
portal from the church of St Dymphne in Gheel (1510),
remains of a carved altar.

Also numerous interesting exhibitions such as:

Brussels tapestries from 1513 (the legend of Erkenbald)
and from 1518 (legend of Notre-Dame-du-Sablon).

Carvings in the style of Louis XV.

Ivory pieces from the 11th to 14th century and objects
created by goldsmiths from the 12th to 18th century.

Enamel pieces from Limoges (13th-century).

Furniture from Louis XV and Louis XVI period.

Clocks and *watches* from the 17th to 19th century.

Tombstones from the 13th to 17th century.

Porcelain with faiences from Antwerp, Delft and Arn-
heim; vase dating from 1562, Chinese porcelain.

Ceramics from Germany, France, England and Belgium; faience pottery from Bernhard Palissy as well as
from the Orient.

Cloth and embroidery: silk, embroidered and painted,
as well as velvet and vestments.

Belgian lace: this collection is one of the most lovely
as well as one of the most complete of its kind.

Lace from Brussels and Brabant in various styles; lace
from Mechelen, Valenciennes, Binche; a coverlet be-
longing to Archduke Albert and his wife Isabella.

Belgian Lace

Autoworld collection

Two special collections in the complex of the Cinquantenaire Palace are the Autoworld which depicts the development of the automobile from 1896–1960 and
includes vehicles which once belonged to prominent personalities; and the Air and Space Museum (Musée de
l'Air/Luchtvaartmuseum) with an overview of manned
flight from its inception up until today.

Route 8B

After leading through Cinquantenaire Park, Avenue
Kennedy changes its name to Avenue de Tervuren/Ter-
vurenlaan. This street, constructed in 1897, leads over
Montgomery Square and across Leopold II Square to the
east. It then turns southeast towards the neighbourhood of
Woluwe-Saint Pierre/Sint Pieters-Woluwe. To the north
of this wide avenue is a congress centre, located on Avenue Charles Thielemans/Karel Thielemanslaan.

The road curves around the northern end of Woluwe
Park (80ha/200 acres) **64** with its several lakes. This park
was planned and executed under King Leopold II. Immediately beyond the railway tracks is a right turn towards
Val Duchesse Abbey. Those not wishing to visit the abbey
should remain on Avenue de Tervuren.

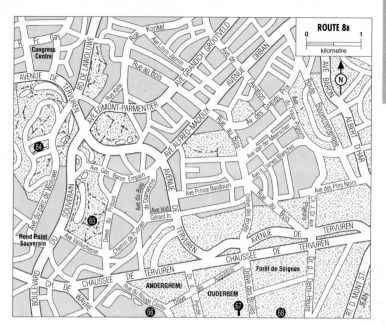

Boulevard du Souverain/Vorstlaan leads between Woluwe Park and the adjacent greens with more ponds south towards the **Val Duchesse Abbey** (Abbaye du Val Duchesse/Abdij van Hertoginnedal) **65**. This was once the home of the oldest Dominican congregation in the Netherlands. It was founded in the 13th century by Duchess Aleyde of Brabant. It was here, back in 1956, that the European experts worked out the text of the founding treaties of the Common Market and Euratom. Near the abbey is the Romanesque St Anne's chapel, dating from the 12th century.

The Val Duchesse Abbey is located in the community of Auderghem/Oudergem which is also home to the Art and Culture Centre (Centre Culturel et Artistique/Kultureel en Artistiek Centrum) further south along Boulevard du Souverain/Vorstlaan. The Abbey of the Red Cloister (Abbaye du Rouge Cloitre/Abdij van het Rode Klooster) **66** is also located in this town, to the south of Chaussée de Tervuren/Tervuurse Steenweg. To continue on to Tervuren from the Val Duchesse Abbey, turn left from Boulevard du Souverain, just south of Rond Point Souverain, onto Chaussée de Wavre/Waversesteenweg. After a few hundred metres, turn left again onto the above-mentioned Chaussée de Tervuren. This merges with Avenue de Tervuren (*see above*) and leads to the town of Tervuren, about 14km (9 miles) away, which is on the road to Leuven (Louvain) and has a castle which houses the Museum of Central Africa.

Abbey of the Red Cloister

Tervuren Castle ⑥⑦. The former domain of the dukes of Brabant was destroyed under orders from Joseph II. In its place, Leopold II built a structure in Louis XVI style. Constructed between 1904–10, it was called the Colonial Museum or the Museum of the Belgian Congo. The ★ **castle park**, 200ha (495 acres) of grounds with French-style gardens, ponds and flower gardens, also houses the tiny St Hubertus chapel, the 18th-century castle stables and the Gordael mill.

The former Colonial Museum is today known as the **Museum of Central Africa** (Musée de l'Afrique Centrale/Museum voor Midden-Afrika). The entrance is at Chaussée de Louvain/Leuvensesteenweg 13. The extensive collections relate to the people of the Central African region – anthropology, history and ethnology – as well as to the geology, mineralogy, botany and zoology of Central Africa. Particularly interesting is the impressive collection of sculptures.

Museum of Central Africa

Just as Routes 8A and 8B can be combined to make a day's outing, it is also possible simply to travel to Tervuren and from there further out into the countryside. One suggestion would be to follow the motorway through the Soignes Woods in a southwesterly direction. This leads, after about 15km (just over 9 miles), to the Battlefield of Waterloo (*see Route 9, page 53*). Another possibility is to take the motorway towards Namur to the southeast for about the same distance, exiting at Rosières. From there it is about 3km (2 miles) south to **Rixensart Castle ⑥⑧** (*see Map, page 49*). Its buildings were constructed around two castle courtyards in the 17th century by the lords of the region, in the elaborate style of the times.

Rixensart Castle courtyard

Route 9

Museums in Ixelles and Southern Brussels – Abbey of Cambre – Bois de la Cambre Woods – Free University – ★★Waterloo – Beersel Castle

The route to the main destination of this tour, Bois de la Cambre, south of the city centre, leaves the boulevard ring at Louise Square on Avenue Louise/Louizalaan. If you are interested in visiting one or more of the museums described below, you should proceed from Porte de Namur (Naamse Poort) along Chaussée de Wavre/Waversesteenweg, making a short detour through the neighbourhood of Ixelles/Elsene.

Shortly thereafter, on the left (Chaussée de Wavre 150), is the **Camille Lemonnier Museum** (Musée Camille Lemonnier) **⑥⑨**. It contains numerous documents from the literary life of this French-Belgian author who was born in Ixelles in 1845 and died there in 1913. He is said to have been a model and patron of the Jeune Belgique Group. His

In the Bois de la Cambre

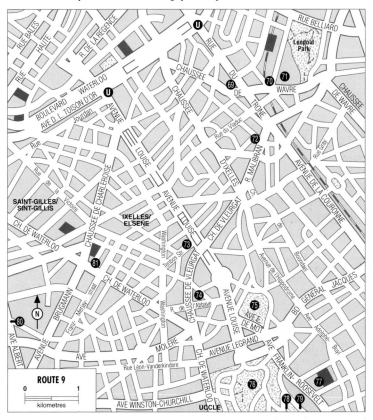

novels describe the life of Belgian workers and peasants in a natural as well as socio-critical style. Continue on Chaussée de Wavre turning left into Rue Vautier/Vautierstraat. At house No 62 is the **Wiertz Museum** ⑩. This is the former atelier of the Belgian Romantic painter Antoine Wiertz (1806–65) and contains most of his works. Wiertz painted numerous large pictures, many with morbid contents, some with pan-optical effects.

Across from the Wiertz Museum, in Leopold Park, is the **Institute of Natural Sciences** (Institut des Sciences Naturelles/Instituut voor Natuurwetenschapen) ⑪. It has 10 departments open to the public including Zoology, Palaeontology, Mineralogy, Palaeobotany, Anthropology and Prehistoric Studies. Chaussée de Wavre makes a sharp right curve at Jourdan Square, heading southeast. At this point the route turns right into Rue Gray. Shortly thereafter is a fork to the right onto Rue du Sceptre/Scepterstraat which leads across Raymond Blykaerts Square to Rue Malibran/Malibraanstraat.

At Rue Jan Van Volsem 71, the road parallel to Rue Malibran, is the **Museum of Fine Arts of Ixelles** (Musée des Beaux-Arts d'Ixelles/Museum voor Schone Kunsten van Elsene) ⑫. The museum contains mainly paintings by French and Belgian Impressionists from the beginning of this century. Volsem and Hennin Street complete this museum detour circle through Ixelles and lead back to Avenue Louise, where the route continues south. On the right is a Children's Museum (Musée des Enfants) ⑬ in Rue de Tenbosch/Tenbosstraat and the **Constantin Meunier Museum** ⑭ at Rue de l'Abbaye/Abdijstraat 59. This house was built by the artist (1831–1905) at the end of the last century and contains about 170 of his sculptures and 120 of his oils, aquarelles and drawings. After 1886, Meunier devoted almost his entire time to sculpting, creating mainly individual figures of people working.

Shortly before the end of Avenue Louis (Louizalaan), at the northern edge of the wooded Bois de la Cambre on the left, is the **Abbey of Cambre** (Abbaye de la Cambre/Ter-Kamerenabdij) ⑮. It commemorates a Cistercian brotherhood founded here in the 13th century, in the middle of the Soignes Woods. Particularly interesting are the late 14th-century Gothic church and the cloisters which were restored in 1934. The abbey seen here today, built in the 18th century under the direction of the Abbess Séraphine de Snoy, is surrounded by French-style gardens. The garden terraces, which are laid out on five different levels, attract large numbers of visitors at the weekends. Today the abbey houses a military academy and Brussels' College of Decorative Arts.

The wooded park of **Bois de la Cambre** (Ter-Kamerenbos) ⑯ is about 500m (1,640ft) wide, 2km (1.2 miles)

Abbey of Cambre
Abbey Gardens

long and encompasses about 100ha (250 acres). It is a part of the former Soignes Woods which was acquired by the city of Brussels in 1842. In about 1860 the landscape architect Keilig turned it into a recreational and amusement park with restaurants and cafés, riding and roller skating paths and rowing boats for hire. The small De Poche Theatre is here in Châlet du Gymnase. On the eastern side of the park is a complex of buildings housing the **Free University of Brussels** (Université Libre de Bruxelles/Vrije Universiteit van Brussel) **77**, founded by Th. Verhaegen in 1834. It also has expansive new buildings 1km further east, on the other side of the tracks and Etterbeek station.

Free University of Brussels

On the western edge of Bois de la Cambre, Chaussée de Water/Waterloose Steenweg leads south from the Soignes Woods to the **★★ Waterloo Battlefield 78**, located about 20km (12 miles) from the city centre (*see Map of surroundings, page 9*). It was here in June 1815 that Napoleon suffered his crushing defeat at the hands of the English, Germans and Dutch under the command of the Duke of Wellington and Blücher.

53

To be precise, the actual battle took place a few kilometres further south at Belle Alliance, but the victorious generals waged their campaign from this point. The almost 40-m (130-ft) high Lion's Hill (Butte du Lion), visible from afar, is crowned by a cast iron monument of a lion. The hill provides a good panorama of the surrounding battlefield.

Lion on the Hill

Visited by approximately 1 million people every year, the battlefield and associated sights is one of the most popular attractions in the entire province of Brabant.

At the foot of the hill, in Braine l'Alleud/Eigenbrakel, is an interesting **Panorama Museum** of the battle. Numerous historic buildings are also preserved, including the Inn of Belle Alliance where Napoleon had his headquar-

Viewing Waterloo Battlefield

ters. A museum is housed in an old inn which served as headquarters for General Wellington. Inscriptions on the church walls recall the fallen multitudes.

Instead of heading directly back to the city, a visit to **Beersel Castle** ⓱ is to be recommended (*see Map, page 51*). This castle, with its three unusual-shaped towers, dates from the early 14th century and is surrounded by a wide moat. After a siege at the end of the 15th century, the castle was partially rebuilt, then restored in 1920.

The return trip to Brussels leads either via the motorway or via the road from Alsemberg. Two more sights lie along this route. At the end of the motorway, at the junction of the highway to Forest/Vorst, between Boulevard de la 2e Armée Britannique/Britse 2e Laégerlaan and Chaussée de Bruxelles/Brusselse Steenweg, is the **Abbey of St-Denis** (Abbaye de St-Denis/Sint-Denijsabdij) ⓰ . There are only a few remains of the original 18th-century abbey. But beside them is the 11th-century church of St-Denis, providing a fine example of the Gothic style from its inception up to the 16th century. The Romanesque chapel of St Alena houses the grave of St Denis.

The road from Alsemberg, the Chaussée d'Alsemberg/Alsembergse Steenweg, leads directly to the southernmost point of the boulevard ring (Porte de Hal). However, it is also possible to turn right beforehand onto Avenue Brugmann/Brugmannlaan, making a short detour. At the end of Avenue Brugmann is the **Horta Museum** ⓱ . The entrance is on Rue Américaine/Amerikastraat. Victor Horta (1861–1947) was one of the most renowned art nouveau architects. He played an important role in the modernisation of 20th-century Belgian architecture.

For fans of art deco, the Tourist Information Office (*see page 96*) has a brochure providing several suggestions for walking tours through the city with this theme.

Art nouveau, Horta Museum

Horta Museum staircase

Route 10

Basilica of the Sacred Heart in Koekelberg – Groot Castle – Bijgaarden – Gaasbeek Castle – Erasmus House

The sights in the western part of Brussels are considerably more spread out than those in the other three outlying sectors of the city. Nevertheless, for those who have time, they are certainly well worth a visit. This is particularly true of the basilica of Koekelberg and the Erasmus House. The route to Koekelberg is easy to find. Leave the boulevard ring at Place Sainctelette and drive along Boulevard Léopold II/Leopold II Laan towards Ghent and Ostend. In the western part of Elisabeth Park this road divides, pass-

Basilica of Koekelberg

55

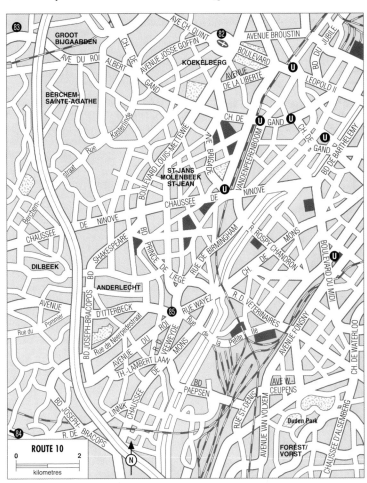

ing on either side of the **Basilique Nationale Sacré-Coeur** (Nationale Basiliek van Het H. Hart) **32** in Koekelberg. Consecrated to the Sacred Heart, it serves as a memorial to all the heroes who gave their lives for their fatherland. Leopold II laid the cornerstone of this 162-m (531-ft) long structure in 1905, but it wasn't until 1970 that the finishing touches were applied. Although it was originally designed as a Gothic building, the layout of the foundation walls was changed in 1926. The apse was completed in 1935 and the basilica consecrated in 1951, despite the fact that construction took a further 19 years to complete. It is said to be one of the largest churches in the world. The modern architecture of the building as well as the lovely stained-glass windows are noteworthy.

Beyond the basilica, the route leaves the E5 motorway to the left via Avenue du Panthéon/Panthéonlaan, turning right at Avenue Josse Goffin/J. Goffinlaan. This turns into Avenue du Roi Albert/Konig Albertlaan, which leads through the neighbourhood of Berchem-Sainte Agathe/Sint Agatha-Berchem to the town of Groot Bijgaarden/Grand Bigard. From here, it follows Brusselstraat

56

Castle of Groot Bijgaarden

to the **Castle of Groot Bijgaarden** (Château de Grand Bigard/Kasteel van Groot Bijgaarden) **33**, located 7km (4 miles) from the city centre. This castle dates from the 16th and 17th century and was completely restored in 1922 by its owners, the Pelgrim family. Because it is still a private residence, it is not open to the public. Particularly interesting, however, is the detached medieval guard tower. The castle museum is well appointed with Renaissance furniture as well as a collection of paintings by old German and Italian Masters.

Another attractive castle is located about 10km (6 miles) further south of here, about 12km (7½ miles) from the city centre. The route to this castle leads over many small unmarked roads, through Sint Martem-Bodegem, across Highway No 9 east of Schepdaal and then into Gaasbeek. The **Castle of Gaasbeek** (Château de Gaasbeek/Kasteel van Gaasbeek) **34**, originally dating from the 13th century, has been renovated on numerous occasions throughout the years. In the 19th century parts of it were totally reconstructed under the direction of the architect Charles Albert. It is renowned as one of the most affluent of all the Brabant castles, with its splendid collection of tapestries and furniture, as well as goldsmith's work, ivory pieces and wood carvings.

Interior, Castle of Gaasbeek

The return route to the centre of Brussels leads first to the city limits via Route de Lennik/Lennikse Baan and then through Anderlecht, the largest community in the southwest of Greater Brussels, straddling both sides of the Charleroi Canal. It follows Chaussée de Mons/Bergens-

Interior of the Erasmus House

esteenweg about 1km further north to Rue de Veeweide/
Veeweydestraat on the left. This leads to the two squares
of Place de la Vaillance/Dapperheidsplein and Square Jef-
Dillen. Here, almost adjacent to one another, are the Eras-
mus House and the church of St Peter and St Guido **35**.
Nearby, in Rue de Chapelein/Kapelaanstraat 1–7, is the
Anderlecht Cultural Centre (Centre Intellectuel/Intel-
lectueel Centrum).

The **Erasmus House** (Maison d'Erasme) in Rue de
Chapitre/Kapitelstraat 31 presents an interesting cross-
section of the life and works of Erasmus of Rotterdam
(1466-1536), who is today generally recognised as the
greatest Humanist of his age. It was here in this patrician
house that Erasmus lodged during his five-month visit
to Brussels in 1521; it belonged to a canon and friend of
his named Pierre Wichman. The rooms, adorned with valuable paintings, still give a good idea of the original furnishings of the period. Well worth seeing is Erasmus's
study, which contains his desk, his armchair, and even
his inkwell and books. His reliquary holds his death mask
and his private seal. The paintings are ascribed to the artists
Quentin Metsys, Albrecht Dürer and Hans Holbein.

Painting in the Erasmus House

The church of **St Peter and St Guido** (Eglise Saints
Pierre et Guidon/HH Pieter en Guidokerk), a Gothic structure with a Romanesque crypt, was constructed between
the 14th and 16th centuries. It boasts a belfry and some
magnificent frescoes.

From here, the return route follows Rue Wayez/Wayezs-
traat which links up with the Chaussée de Mons/Bergens-
esteenweg after having crossed over the canal at E.v.d.
Velde Square.

St Peter and St Guido

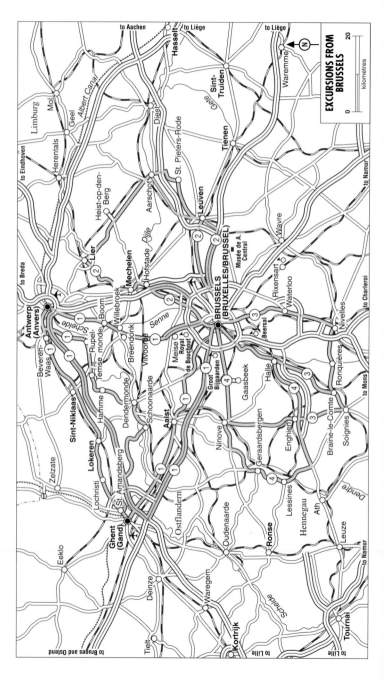

Excursion 1

★★ Antwerp – Sint Niklaas – Lokoren – Rupelmonde – ★★ Ghent – Aalst (170km/105 miles)

The central location of the Belgian capital makes it an ideal starting point for both longer and shorter excursions into all parts of the country. This book has limited its selection to a zone of 50km (30 miles) around Brussels, suggesting sights that can be reached easily on a day trip.

The first excursion leads the visitor north and northwest through Brabant to the Flemish provinces of Antwerp and East Flanders. Rather than taking the main thoroughfare to Antwerp via Mechelen (this city is covered in Excursion 2, *see page 66*), the route suggested here is via Vilvoorde-Breendonk-Boom (*see Map, page 58*). This provides the opportunity to visit the baroque abbey church of Grimbergen west of Vilvoorde as well as the Domäne Bouchout in Miese, both of which are described in Route 7 (*see page 40*).

Mechelen

61

This route leaves Brussels on the N1, travelling alongside the Canal de Willebroek, also known as the Sea Canal. It leads mainly through industrialised regions before turning left in Vilvoorde onto the N211. This leads via Grimbergen to the A12 north of Meise. This motorway can, of course, also be taken directly from Brussels. About 10km (6 miles) north from Meise is the town of **Breendonk**. The town's fort served as a concentration camp and was converted to a national museum in 1948. To visit the museum, follow the signs to Fort Breendonk (not to the town of Breendonk). Just past Breendonk is Willebroek, the town which gave the canal its name. The next town, **Boom** is the centre of the Rupel region and, with its clay-rich soil, Belgium's most important brick region. The canal joins the Rupel river here.

★★ Antwerp

The capital of the province of Antwerp is situated 50km (31 miles) north of Brussels and has a population of 270,000 (680,000 including the suburbs). Although Antwerp is almost 90km (55 miles) from the open sea, it is Belgium's most important port. The harbour is on the Scheldt river which is, at Antwerp, 550m (1,800ft) wide and 9–13m (30–43ft) deep. The old town, on the east banks of the river, is surrounded by a 6-km (4-mile) long boulevard built in 1859 to replace the 16th-century Spanish city wall. Almost all of the sights of interest are located in this part of Antwerp. The most noteworthy sight on the outskirts of the city is the **Castle Steen**, on the banks of the Scheldt, which houses a ★ **maritime museum**. The oldest parts of this fortress date from the 9th century while

Castle Steen Maritime Museum

Meat Hall Museum

Folk Culture exhibit

Cathedral of Our Dear Lady

the rest of the city wall was built in 1225. The departure point for ships which take visitors on tours of the harbour is near the castle.

The best place to begin a tour of the city centre is at the Late Gothic ★ **Meat Hall** (Vleeshuis), built in the 16th century to serve as a butchers' market hall and guild hall. The butchers' meeting room is noteworthy. Today the building houses a local museum with archaeological finds and artistic crafts. It is just a short distance from here to the Grand' Place with the **Town Hall** (Stadhuis), built in 1561–5 in Renaissance style, renovated in the 19th century. Inside there are some interesting murals depicting the history of the city.

In Gildenkamerstraat, which leads off the square, is the **Museum of Folk Culture**, founded in 1907, which provides an extensive overview of the folk art of Flanders. The ★★ **Cathedral of Our Dear Lady** (Onze Lieve-Vrouwe-Kerk) is south of the museum, on Handschoenmarkt. It is not only Belgium's largest church but is also one of the largest Gothic churches in the world. Construction was begun in the early 14th century but was not completed until the 17th century. The 123-m (404-ft) high north steeple was built in the 16th century while the southern steeple was never completed. The impressive interior contains works by Rubens as well as spectacular stained-glass windows and a glockenspiel with 47 chimes. The largest bell, that with the deepest tone, weighs 8 tons. From the cathedral, the tour leads through Korte Nieuwstraat to Hendrik-Conscienceplein with its ★ **St Carolus Borromeus Kerk**, built in 17th-century baroque style.

The church, which boasts a lovely facade as well as elegant steeples, was damaged by fire in 1718. The Rubens Chapel, however, was spared from the flames. A wealth of art treasures and a collection of old lace can be seen in the museum of the church.

Interior of St Carolus Borromeus Kerk

The tour now returns to Korte Nieuwstraat and continues along Lande Nieuwstraat leading to the **Burgundian chapel** which dates from the 15th century. The arches and murals are noteworthy. Just a bit further along the same street is the Late Gothic (15th/16th-century) ★ **St Jacobs Kerk** with its unfinished steeple. Its interior is decorated with a wide variety of art treasures including sculptures, paintings, crafted objects of silver and gold, embroidery, manuscripts and robes. The Rubens' burial chapel is situated in the choir.

Continuing along Nieuwstraat, the route crosses the broad ring boulevard at Franklin Roosevelt Square. This boulevard was built along the lines of the former city wall. To the right, in Langen Herentalsestraat, is the **Antwerp World Diamond Centre** where a display depicts a diamond's path from the time it is mined to the time it becomes a finished jewel or industrial diamond. The main railway station is on a cross-street further to the east.

Antwerp Diamond Centre

Behind this is the **Zoo** with its Museum of Natural History, planetarium, aquarium, delphinarium, nocturama (with nocturnal animals), aviary and reptile house.

The zoo is the easternmost point of the city tour which now leads through the lively shopping street De Keyserlei. Following Frankrijklei, the route leads through Leysstraat to the broad connecting street of Meir. Rubensstraat branches off this street and is the site of the ★ **Rubens House** built by the Flemish painter in 1610. He lived here until his death in 1640. Aside from the magnificently appointed interior, the house also has an impressive portico in the courtyard.

The Rubens House

At the end of Rubensstraat, Schuttershofstraat leads to the right. Follow this to Lange Gasthuisstraat where the ★ **Mayer van den Bergh Museum**, with one of Belgium's most important collections, is located. The *Dulle Griet* by Pieter Brueghel the Elder is the main attraction of the collection of paintings. Additionally, the museum houses a rich collection of sculptures from the 6th to 18th century, gold and silver objects and lace and embroidery.

On the same street, a bit further along, is the **Maagdenhuis**, constructed partially in 1564 and partially in 1635. This former girls' orphanage has a lovely facade. Paintings, sculptures and decorative pieces, including 16th-century Antwerp faience pottery, are found in the small museum here. Continuing through Lange and Korte Gasthuisstraat, the route turns left and leads through Lombardenvest and Steenhouwervest to ★ **Plantin Moretus**

Bust of Plantin Moretus

Museum on Vrijdagmarkt. This Renaissance structure was used by the printer Plantin in the 16th century as his workshop. It continued in use as a workshop until 1876 and is today preserved in its original form including typographic equipment and materials.

Hoogstraat links the nearby St Jansvliet Square (entrance to Scheldt pedestrian tunnel) to the main square.

There are several different routes which lead from Antwerp south to Ghent. If you are short of time take the A14 motorway. If you have more time and want to become acquainted with the countryside and the people outside of the large cities, follow the old Route 14 north of the motorway through Sint Niklaas. Another alternative is to take small roads which follow alongside the Scheldt. All of these routes cross the provincial border into East Flanders just a few kilometres west of Antwerp.

The first Flemish town along Route 14 is known as the Town of Lace, **Beveren-Waas**. Charming, tree-lined lanes lead to the Cortewalle Castle and the church with its richly-decorated interior. It was built in the Gothic style of the Scheldt region.

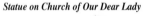

Sint Niklaas (population of 68,300) is the major town in the densely populated and fertile Waas region. Its main square spreads over more than 3ha (7 acres). This is the location of the neo-Gothic Town Hall (1876) with a glockenspiel in the tower, the church of St Niklaas, built in the 15th and 16th century and often restored and expanded in later years, as well as numerous other interesting buildings. One of these is the Parochiehuis, built in 1663 and originally used as a vicarage before being converted to the Town Hall. Today it houses the courts. Another of the buildings is the Ciperage, built in 1662 as a prison. Today it serves as the library. Here, too, is the Landhuis, built in 1637. Behind the Town Hall is the towering church of Our Dear Lady, the steeple of which is crowned by a gilt statue of Mary.

Church of St Niklaas

Statue on Church of Our Dear Lady

Lokoren (population 28,000) is 15km (9 miles) further, south of Route 14. The church of St Lawrence here has a carved pulpit dating from 1736. Twelve kilometres (7 miles) further is **Lochristi**, a town stretching along both sides of the road. From the end of July until September, the aroma of flowers is in the air as the begonia fields which this area is renowned for, spreading over 125ha (310 acres), come alive in a magnificent burst of colour. The road continues on towards Ghent through St Amandsberg whose cemetery is the last resting place of numerous prominent Flemish personalities from the world of art, culture and science.

For those who select the southern route which leaves Antwerp via Burcht on the Scheldt, the following sights are of interest.

Rupelmonde is a centuries-old sailing and fishing village, and birthplace of the geographer Mercator. This famous 16th-century Belgian, who is portrayed on the country's 1,000 franc note, was held prisoner in the moated castle here. The tower still stands and serves today as a museum of the Scheldt. A monument to Mercator stands in front of the church of St Mary. The town, home to the Scheldt's only tidal mill, also has, in the cellar of the Scaldiana Guesthouse, a diorama of this river.

The route now leads through the shipbuilding village of Temse with its noteworthy paintings and carvings in the church and wonderful eel specialities in the restaurants along the wharf. Next comes Hamme, where a swampy region called De Bunt, lying between the river and the Durme valley, contains a wealth of interesting flora and fauna. The route continues through **Dendermond**, whose Palace of Justice tower is decorated by a bronze horse. The sights worth seeing in this city of 42,000 people include the Town Hall with its bell tower in the main square, the Museum of Antiquity and Ethnology in the former meat hall and the interior of the church of St Mary with its wealth of art treasures.

Continuing on through Schoonaarde and Overmere (site of a Museum of the Peasants' Revolt) and, via a short detour, through Laarne with its impressive moated castle, the road now leads to the capital of East Flanders, located just under 60km (37 miles) from Antwerp.

★★ Ghent

In the Middle Ages, Ghent (population 100,000, with suburbs 230,000) was the capital of the cloth trade. Today, it is still the textile industry as well as the metal industry which makes Ghent an important commercial centre. Despite its inland location, the city is the country's second largest port owing to the canal link to Westerscheldt and

Museum of Antiquity and Ethnology

65

Mercator monument

Palace of Justice tower

thus to the North Sea. Numerous structures from past centuries are preserved in Ghent, making a visit to the town centre well worthwhile.

The main attractions are concentrated in an almost circular area with a diameter of 1km around the Town Hall and the cloth hall. On the west side of the Botermarkt is the three-storey ★ **Town Hall** (Stadhuis) with a facade decorated with Doric, Ionic and Corinthian pillars. Its Gothic portions date from the 16th century while the Renaissance parts are from the 17th century.

Across from the Town Hall is the **Cloth Hall** (Lakenhalle) built in 1425. Its 95-m (310-ft) bell tower dates from the 14th century. A lift takes you to the top where a spectacular view of the city is the reward. Almost all of the 52 bells date from the year 1660.

On the square in front of this building are the Youths Fountain and the Triomfante Bell.

St Michael's Church

Passing by the huge St Nicholas Church (13th-century), the route leads to the Koornmarkt with a variety of houses dating from the 16th and 17th century. It then leads around the post office and to St Michael's Bridge, crossing over the Leie to **St Michael's Church** which was begun in 1440 and completed in the 17th century. The steeple remains unfinished. Returning across the bridge towards the Koornmarkt, the path follows Graslei Street along the banks of the Leie. The old guild halls lining this street are particularly lovely.

Museum for Decorative Arts

Recrossing the Leie via Grasbrug, the route reaches the **Museum for Decorative Arts and Industrial Design** in Jan Breydelstraat. Here, in an old patrician house, a rich collection, including period furniture, is on display.

On the left side of Burgstraat are several beautifully ornamented and graduated gables. The route now turns to the right, crossing the Leie once again, and leading to one of the main attractions, the old castle fortress of the Counts of Flanders, ★ **'s Gravensteen**. Built between 1180 and 1200 on the foundation of a 10th-century structure, it was thereafter expanded and renovated numerous times over the years. Today it is one of the best preserved medieval fortresses in Europe. Its walls, rising up out of the river, contain 24 pinnacled towers.

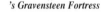

's Gravensteen Fortress

From St Veerleplein (to the left on the riverside street, Kraanlei is the local museum), the route crosses over the Leie bridge and Groentenmarkt, leading through Hoogpoort to the Town Hall. Anyone especially interested in church architecture might want to walk about 300m (985ft) down Borluutstraat to visit St Jacob's Church, completed in the 17th century. It has a Romanesque portal (12th-century) and a tabernacle dating from 1593. Also, behind the Cloth Hall, and a few steps down St Baafsplein is ★ **St Bavo's Cathedral**, which was built between the 10th and 16th centuries. It has a 12th-century Romanesque crypt and a 89-m (282-ft) high steeple.

The most valuable treasure here is the renowned Ghent altarpiece, the *Adoration of the Holy Lamb* (1420–32) by the van Eyck brothers. It is reputed to be one of the most important examples of medieval painting. Numerous other treasures make the interior of this cathedral a veritable museum of sculpture, wrought iron, carving and painting.

Pulpit in St Bavo's

The 55-km (34-mile) return trip from Ghent to Brussels can be made via the A10 motorway linking Ostend to the capital. For those with a bit more time, however, an alternative route along the N9 can be recommended, with a pause in Aalst. The entire excursion can be shortened by eliminating the trip to Ghent and heading south directly from Dendermonde (*see page 63*) to **Aalst**. This town (population 79,000) is situated on the Dender and is famous both as an industrial city and as a centre for cut flowers. The interesting sights are grouped around the market place with its monument to Dirk Martens. It was he who founded the first printing shop of the United Netherlands here. In the interior courtyard of the Gothic Town Hall is a country house in rococo style. The bell tower houses a glockenspiel. Two other interesting sights here are the never-completed St Martin's church constructed in Brabant High Gothic style with a marble tabernacle dating from 1605; and the Rubens painting *St Rochus and the Plague-Infested*.

The road back to Brussels is lined on both sides with rolling hills and hop fields. Passing through the small village of Hekelgem, note the two old windmills, both of which are historic preservation sites.

67

Ghent Altarpiece, St Bavo's

Excursion 2

★★ Mechelen – ★★ Lier – Aarschot – Leuven (115km/71 miles)

Just as in the first excursion, this route leads north from Brussels, either along the A1 motorway (E19) or the N1 towards Antwerp. It exits, however, at Mechelen-Zuid. If you choose the N1, make a stop at the national domain **Hofstade**, an expansive recreational centre with several ponds and 80ha (200 acres) of beach. Two larger lakes provide opportunities for a wide variety of water sports. The park also contains a bird preserve.

★★ *Mechelen*

This town of 76,000 inhabitants is presided over by the 97-m (318-ft) high Gothic steeple of ★ **St Rombout's Cathedral** (good panorama). The steeple, begun in 1452 and completed in 1578, was originally designed to reach a height of 168m (551ft). It turned into a colossal stump, however, when William of Orange appropriated the necessary building materials for the construction of the Willemstad fortress. The tower has one of Belgium's most beautiful glockenspiels, with 49 bells. The cathedral itself was built mainly in the 13th and 14th century. The interior is in baroque style. It houses the renowned painting by Van Dyck, *Christ on the Cross* (1627), the tombs of two cardinals, a baroque statue of the first archbishop of Mechelen, Cardinal Granvella and the burial chapel of Cardinal Mercier (1851–1926).

Christ on the Cross by Van Dyck

The Grote Markt

The focal point of the city is the **Grote Markt**, lined with Renaissance and baroque houses. On the south side is the **Cloth Hall**, modelled on that in Bruges and dating from the 14th century. Here, too, is the former Schepenhuis (city council building), today the Town Hall. Another important building, to the east of the Grote Markt, is the Palace of Justice. This was once the residence of the city ruler, Margaret of Austria, as well as of Cardinal Granvella. The building was constructed from 1503–7. Its Renaissance facade was fashioned between 1517–26.

Also in Mechelen is the 15th-century **St John's Church** with an important altarpiece by Rubens, *The Adoration of the Magi*. In the southern part of the city, the noteworthy Brussels Gate with its double tower is worth seeing. This is the only remaining one of the 12 city gates.

The tour continues north via Duffel, where it crosses the Nete, to ★★ **Lier** (population 31,000).

Brussels Gate

This town was popularised by the writings of Felix Timmerman (1886–1947). His books have been translated into 24 languages. Sights of note here are the 18th-century Town Hall with a bell tower from 1369, the oldest Beguine convent in the Netherlands, founded in the 13th century, and the so-called **Zimmer** or **Cornelius Tower**. The tower, originally a part of the city wall, got its name from the Lier watch-maker and astronomer Zimmer, the creator of the tower's fantastic astronomic clock.

The late-Gothic structure of St Gommarus is also noteworthy. Its 80-m (260-ft) high tower, with glockenspiel, is said to have the shape of a pepper shaker.

Aarschot is the next destination on the route. The old ducal grain mills, the church of St Mary's, a Gothic masterpiece, and the Beguine convent are of interest here.

Zimmer Tower and clock

★★ Leuven/Louvain

This city of 85,000 residents was already home to a large number of weavers in the 13th and 14th century, making it an important European textile centre. Additionally, a university was founded here in 1425. Although the city was severely damaged during the war, the market place's two main attractions, the Late Gothic Town Hall and St Peter's Church, did not suffer any lasting effects.

The ★★ **Town Hall** (Stadhuis) was built by M de Layens from 1448–63. With its towers, arched windows and spectacularly moulded facade, this building is one of the most beautiful examples of medieval architecture. The detached facades are composed of three storeys of Gothic arched windows. On the four corners and above the front and rear gables, six slender towers protrude like the masts of a ship. The reliefs are particularly elaborate and depict scenes from the Old and New Testament.

St Peter's Church is also a late-Gothic structure (begun in 1425). Its exterior was never completed because the ground on which it stands was too soft. The west steeple was thus never built. In the expansive interior of the church, the 12-m (39-ft) high sanctuary as well as the rood screen (1450) were executed by de Layens, the architect who designed the Town Hall. The most valuable treasures of the church, however, are the two paintings by Dirk Bouts, who lived in Leuven and died there in 1475. These are the *Martyrdom of St Erasmus* and his masterpiece, created between 1464–8 for the sacrament chapel, *The Last Supper Altar*.

The magnificent baroque facade of **St Michael's Church** symbolises the triumph of the Counter-Reformation. Other sights of note in Leuven are the Gothic St Gertrude's church and the Parck Abbey, situated outside the city. This Premonstratensian monastery was founded in 1129. The buildings seen there today date from the 17th and 18th century.

From Leuven it is about 25km (16 miles) back to Brussels either along the A3 motorway, the N2 (via Zaventem) or the N3 via Tervuren.

69

Town Hall facade

St Michael's Church

Excursion 3

★ Nivelles – ★ Ronquières – Soignies – Halle (95km/59 miles)

Excursions 3 and 4 both lead south and southwest, which means that they can be combined easily into one longer excursion. Leaving Brussels on the N5, the route leads south towards Waterloo, continuing on the N27 past the Lion's Hill. On the right side, just before reaching the city, is the race track of Nivelles-Baulers (Autodrome).

★ **Nivelles** (population 22,000) was one of Belgium's most picturesque historic cities, before it was badly damaged during World War II. It grew up around a nuns' abbey and was, up until the 17th century, one of the cloth cities of Belgium.

St Gertrude's Abbey

The **abbey** in question is dedicated to **St Gertrude**. Founded in the 7th century, it is the oldest such establishment in Belgium. According to legend, following the death of the Frankish ruler Pepin the Elder, his widow Itta retired with their daughter Gertrude to a villa on the hillside overlooking the Thines Valley. After the death of her mother and a deteriorating marriage to Dagobert I, Gertrude founded the monastery, at the instigation of Amand, Bishop of Maastricht. Immediately she set about ordering books from Rome and summoned monks from Ireland. Nowadays, the abbey church, which dates from the 11th century, is regarded as one of the finest Romanesque churches in the country. It was completely burned in 1940 but was reconstructed in its original form.

St Gertrude's cloisters

The porch is flanked by two small towers, the Tour Madame and the Tour de Jean de Nivelles. The copper figure of Jean de Nivelles on the right steeple strikes the time and has become the city's landmark. It was donated by the Duke of Burgundy, Charles the Bold. The cloisters date from the 13th century.

On the Sunday after St Michael's day, Nivelles is the scene of a procession during which the remains of St Gertrude are carried 12km (7 miles) through the city and surrounding area. This tradition has been preserved since the 12th century.

Apart from the abbey, the church and monastery of St Francis, as well as the Museum of Antiquities and the Dodaine Park are all worth a visit.

The route continues west from Nivelles along the N49 to an especially fascinating sight for anyone interested in technology. This is the ★ **Boat lift of Ronquières** on the Charleroi-Brussels Canal. This lift for barges of up to 1,350 tons went into operation here in 1968. It can lift or lower barges 68m (223ft) in one step. The barge drives into a steel lock measuring 90m (295ft) in length and 12m (39ft) in width. The lock, on 236 wheels, is pulled up (or let down) an incline measuring 1,430m (4,692ft) in length. The entire process takes 25 minutes and can be observed from the street bridge. An even better observation point, however, is from the 125-m (410-ft) high control tower (which fortunately has a lift). This construction, which replaced 28 locks, reduces from 35 to 14 hours the time a ship needs to travel the 70km (43 miles) between Charleroi and Brussels.

71

Further west is Braine-le-Comte with a church dating from the 13th–16th century and a Renaissance Town Hall. Continuing another 7km (4 miles), the route reaches **Soignies** (population 23,400) with the cloister church of St Vincent. The cloister was donated by St Vincent, husband of St Waltraut, in 653. The only part of the original complex still surviving is the early Romanesque church (10th–11th century). The altar of this church contains a shrine with the bodily remains of Saint Vincent. His head is in another shrine in the choir. Soignies is also the scene of a procession, every Pentecost Sunday, which winds its way along 15km (9 miles). The city is noted for its nearby bluestone quarry, which provides the material to construct many buildings in the Netherlands.

Processional giant,
Braine-le-Comte

St Vincent's Church

From Soignies, two alternatives present themselves. One is to take the N57 north for 12km (7 miles) to Enghien/Edingen when Excursion 4 can be joined. The other is to return to Brussels via **Halle**, described in Excursion 4 (page 70). From here a short detour will lead to the moated Beersel Castle (described in *Route 9, page 51*).

Excursion 4

Halle – Enghien/Edingen – Lessines – Geraardsbergen – Ninove (100km/62 miles)

This, the last excursion, can easily be combined with Excursion 3, as mentioned above (*see Map, page 58*). The city of **Halle**, with a population of 30,000, is a bit less than 20km (12 miles) from the centre of Brussels and thus seems more like a suburb. It can be reached either by leaving the motorway A7/E19 (towards Mons) at the Halle exit or via the N6. If taking the motorway, it is also possible to get off one exit earlier, in Hutzingen, in order to visit the nearby provincial domain of the same name. Its 90ha (222 acres) have been converted to a recreational park and the old castle now houses a restaurant.

Basilica of Our Lady

Halle is well known as a place of pilgrimage where large processions take place annually at Pentecost and on the first Sunday in September.

The town, which is very close to the Flemish/Walloon linguistic border, has a Gothic Basilica of Our Lady, a Flemish Renaissance Town Hall (Stadhuis) dating from 1616, with a bell tower and a baroque former Jesuit college. The latter now serves as the town's cultural centre and tourist information office. The Basilica of Our Lady, built in 1341–1467 and formerly known as the church of St Martin, is a fine example of Brabant Gothic architecture. The tower recalls the fortified towers of many Belgian town halls and weavers' halls. The church houses an alabaster Renaissance altar by Jehan Mone, constructed in the chapel north of the choir in 1533, as well as a carved wooden figure of Mary above the high altar. This figure is said to have miraculous powers and has been the destination of pilgrimages since the year 700. A statue of Mary on the west portal was damaged by cannon fire in 1580 during an unsuccessful attempt by the Calvinists to lay siege to the town.

Enghien town centre

Enghien Park

Continuing along the N8 from Halle, the route leads west and soon crosses the boundary between the provinces of Brabant and Hainaut. The bilingual town of **Enghien/Edingen** (population 4,500) lies directly on this boundary. The castle of the dukes of Enghien, destroyed during the French Revolution, was located in the park of the dukes of Arenberg. The park, which is only sometimes open to the public, stretches across 324ha (800 acres) and contains numerous busts and statues. The alabaster tomb of the Archbishop of Toledo, Wilhelm von Croy, an important work of the Renaissance era, is found in the Capuchin monastery church.

From Enghien/Edingen it is possible to shorten this excursion (by about 20km/12 miles) by driving directly north to Ninove along the N255 or by following the route described in Excursion 3 in the opposite direction, on the N55, which can be reached in Soignies. If you do not wish to shorten the excursion, continue along the N7 to Bassily. From here a small road leads to **Lessines** on the Dender. A narrow, winding road leads from the market place to a lovely square lined with linden trees. This is the site of the church which has four aisles in addition to the nave. Nearby is the museum of the Notre Dame à la Rose, with its marvellous collection of furniture, copper and pewter objects and wrought-iron works.

Lessines Church

The route now leads northeast through the Dender valley, sometimes approaching the river, sometimes meandering away from it. The next town is **Geraardsbergen** where a replica of the Brussels Manneken Pis is found on the outdoor steps of the Town Hall (with four corner towers). Other sights of interest are the fountain in the market place and the 110-m (360-ft) high Oudenberg mountain. A climb to the summit is highly recommended for a spectacular view across the Dender valley. The remains of the former St Adrian's Abbey are now the site of a tourist centre with amusement park and zoo.

Ninove, also situated on the banks of the Dender, is the final stop on this excursion. The Koeport Gate is a remnant of the city wall. The Church of St Mary here has a noteworthy baroque interior with monumental confessionals and lovely wood panelling.

On the return trip to Brussels, it is possible to detour to the Gaasbeek Castle (*see page 56*).

Geraardsbergen from above

73

The Church of St Mary

Art History

It was not until the 12th and 13th century, when it began to thrive commercially, accompanied by a flourish of building activity, that Brussels really began to develop its own art and culture.

Europe's best sculptors and artists were employed to adorn Brussels. The achievements of the master masons and architects are preserved for posterity in the city's buildings. One of the prime examples of this is the Gothic cathedral of St Michael. Construction was begun in 1226 and carried on over several centuries. Among the secular Gothic structures in Brussels, nowhere are the mason's skills better reflected than in the the 15th-century Town Hall. The left wing and the lower section of the tower were built between 1402–20. The tower, which soars to a height of 91 metres (291ft) above the market place, was completed between 1449–55. From 1515, work continued on the King's House opposite. Most of the buildings on the Grand' Place were reconstructed after the French attacks of 1695, with splendid baroque facades.

Detail on the Grand' Place

75

More benign French influence on the city included the construction by Barnabé Guimard of the church of St James on the Coudenberg in 1776 and the Palace of the Council of Brabant (1778–83), which later became the parliament building. Renaissance and neoclassical architecture, well represented throughout Belgium, is best evidenced in Brussels by the buildings around Place Royale, the Stock Exchange and the Palace of Justice.

Sculpture on the Stock Exchange

Innovative architecture, created during the 19th century to reflect the new age of the bourgeoisie included the greenhouse of the Botanical Garden constructed by Tillman-Frans Suys in 1826. Built in 1846, the Galeries Saint-Hubert by Jean-Pierre Chuisenaer was the first covered shopping arcade in Europe. The influence of the emergent working classes at the end of the 19th century is reflected in the Maison du Peuple (People's House) commissioned by the trades unions from the architect Victor Horta. Together with Henry van de Velde, Horta is regarded as one of the leading exponents of art nouveau architecture in Belgium. He constructed trend-setting apartment houses and hotels of stone and cast iron. One such building is the house of the cloth merchant Waucquez, which since 1989 has been the home of the Comic Museum.

Outside the Galeries Saint-Hubert

One of the most renowned masters of Flemish painting, Rogier van der Weyden, settled in Brussels and remained there until his death in 1464. His style was propagated thereafter by other artists including Colijn de Coter. Brussels was also home to many acclaimed wood carvers during this era. A number of their works, the famed Brussels carved altars, were exported to Germany and Sweden.

Brueghel's Dulle Griet

Rubens: Mary visits Elisabeth

In the 16th century, Barend van Orley was responsible for a renewed heyday of painting in Brussels, introducing the Renaissance to the city. And last but not least, one of Belgium's most famous artists, Pieter Brueghel, (1520–69) although born in the village of Brueghel, lived in Brussels for much of his life.

At the same time, Brussels was developing into the centre of European tapestry making, which first became established in the city in the 15th century. Records show that the art of rug weaving was handed down through a number of families from generation to generation throughout the 16th to 18th century. Thus the history of the Brussels Gobelin tapestry trade complements the development of Flemish painting. Beginning with the Late Gothic style, so important at the Burgundian court, Flemish art continues on through the Renaissance, with its Italian influence, all the way to the baroque style, as evidenced by the ecstatic animation shown in the paintings of Peter Paul Rubens.

Thereafter, the decline of Belgian painting began, a trend which was to continue until 1816 when the Frenchman Jacques-Louis David settled in Brussels. In the late 19th to early 20th century, it once again flourished with the advent of artists such as the Surrealist, Paul Delvaux who lived and worked mostly in Brussels and who was influenced by the most famous visionary of them all, René Magritte. While living and working in Brussels, Magritte painted a number of murals for Belgian public buildings. His major paintings include *The Wind and The Song* and *The Human Condition*. An entire room in the Museum of Modern Art is devoted to Magritte's work.

Museums and Collections

Air and Space Museum (Musée de l'Air/Luchtvaart-
museum), Parc du Cinquantenaire/Jubelpark 3. Tuesday
to Sunday 9am–noon and 1–4.45pm. The history of civil-
ian and military flight from 1912 to the present. *Metro:
Merode (line 1); Bus 20, 28, 36, 61, 67, 80; Tram 81.*

Army and Military History Museum (Musée Royal de
l'Armée et d'Histoire Militaire/Koninklijk Museum van
het Leger en Militarie Geschiedenis), Parc du Cinquan-
tenaire/Jubelpark 3. Tuesday to Sunday 9am–noon and
1–4.45pm. The exhibits include drums, trumpets, weapons
and uniforms from the Middle Ages right up to post-World
War II. *Metro: Merode (line 1); Bus: 20, 28, 36, 61, 67,
8; Tram: 81.*

The Atomium

Atomium, Heysel/Heizel, Boulevard du Centenaire/
Eeuwfeestlaan. Exhibition: daily 9.30am–6pm; observation platform: May to August daily 9.30am–10pm. Permanent exhibition *Pioneering in Medicine*. Audio-visual
displays of the latest developments in the world of medicine. *Metro: Heizel (line 1A); Tram 18, 81.*

Vintage models

Autoworld (Wereldpaleis van de Automobiel), Wereldpaleis, Jubelpark 11/Palais Mondial, Cinquantenaire. April
to September daily 10am–6pm; November to March daily
10am–5pm. *Metro: Merode (line 1); Bus 20, 28, 36, 61,
67, 80; Tram 81.*

Beersel Castle (Châteaux/Kasteel). 1 March to 15 November daily 10am–noon and 2–6pm; 16 November to 28
February weekends and holidays only 2–5pm. Interesting
medieval castle with a moat.

In the Botanical Garden

National Botanical Garden of Belgium (Jardin Botan-
ique/Plantentuin), Domäne Bouchout/Domein van Bouchout, in Meise (14km/9 miles) north of Brussels. Park:
daily 9am–sunset; greenhouses: November to Easter Monday to Thursday 1–4pm; Easter to October Monday–
Thursday and Sunday 2–6pm. The 93-ha (230-acre) gardens contain 13 greenhouses full of tropical and subtrop-
ical plants.

Brewery Museum (Musée de la Brasserie/Brouwerij-
museum), Grand' Place/Grote Markt 10. Monday to Friday 10am–noon and 2–5pm; April to October additionally
Saturday 10am–noon. The museum gives the layman a
peek into the techniques of this traditional craft. Kegs and
tools are also exhibited.

Book Museum (Musée de Livre/Museum van het Boek),
located in the Albert I Library, Bd de l'Empereur/Keiz-
erslaan 4. Monday, Wednesday, Saturday 2–5pm; closed
last week of August and public holidays. The fascinating history of book production is depicted with examples from many different periods. *Bus 71, 95, 96; Tram
92, 93, 94.*

Camille Lemonnier Museum (Musée Camille Lemonnier), Chaussée de Wavre/Waversesteenweg 150, Ixelles. Wednesday 1–3pm, Tuesday and Thursday by appointment; closed July and August. Numerous documents and memorabilia provide an overview of the life of the author C Lemonnier. *Metro: Naamse Poort (line 2); Bus 34, 54, 80.*

Charlier Museum, Avenue des Arts/Kunstlaan 16, St Joost. Monday to Friday 1–5pm. Paintings, furniture and dishes from the 19th century. *Metro: Madou or Kunst-Wet (line 1, 2); Bus 29, 37, 60, 63, 65, 66.*

Chinese Pavilion (Pavillon Chinois/Chinese Paviljoen), Avenue Jules van Praet 44, Laeken/J v Praetlaan 44. Tuesday to Friday 9.30am–12.30pm and 1.30–4.45pm, Saturday and Sunday 1.30–3.30pm. Chinese porcelain and objects from Oriental cultures. *Tram 52, 92.*

Constantin Meunier Museum (Musée de Constantin Meunier), Rue de l'Abbaye/Abdijstraat 59, Ixelles. Tuesday to Sunday 10am–noon and 1–5pm. The collection contains pictures by this artist as well as other personal objects. *Tram 23, 90, 93, 9; Bus 38.*

Meet them in the Comic Museum

Comic Museum, Rue des Sables/Zandstraat 20. Tuesday to Sunday 10am–6pm. This collection is dedicated to the heroes of the world of comics, including Hergé's famous character, Tintin. Housed in an especially fine example of Flemish art nouveau architecture by Victor Horta. *Metro: Rogier, Botanique/ Kruidtuin; Bus 38; Tram 52, 55, 58, 81, 90, 92, 93.*

Dynasty Museum (Musée de la Dynastie/Museum v d Dynastie), Rue de Bréderode, Brederodestraat 21. Wednesday and Saturday 2–5pm. The busts of the Belgian rulers are not the only objects in this fascinating collection which brings the history of the country to life. *Metro: Luxembourg; Tram 92, 93, 94; Bus 20, 34, 71, 95, 96.*

The Erasmus House

Erasmus House (Maison d'Erasme/Erasmushuis), Rue du Chapitre/Kapitelstraat 31, Anderlecht. Daily 10am–noon and 2–5pm, except Tuesday and Friday. The works of Erasmus and a small collection of paintings by Holbein, Dürer, David and Bosch, are on display. *Metro: Saint Guido (line 1B); Tram 103; Bus 47, 49.*

Film Museum (Musée du Cinema), Rue Baron Horta/Baron Hortastraat 9. Daily 5.30–10.30pm. The history of film from Chinese shadow plays to the Lumière brothers. Five films are shown daily. *Metro: Central Station (line 1); Tram 92, 93, 94; Bus 20, 29, 38, 60, 63, 65, 66, 71, 95, 96.*

Gaasbeek Castle, coat-of-arms

Gaasbeek Castle, (Chateau de Gaasbeek/Kasteel van Gaasbeek) 12km (7½ miles) from the city. July to August daily 10am–5pm; April to October closed Monday and Friday. This medieval castle houses an art collection as well as works of wrought iron.

Groot Bijgaarden Castle (Château de Grand Bigard/Kasteel van Groot Bijgaarden, 7km (4 miles) from the city centre. Easter weekend to last Sunday in September Sunday and holidays 2–7pm.

Historium 200 Wax Museum, Anspach Centre (1st floor), Anspachlaan 26. Daily 10am–6pm. Two millennia of Belgian history, with prominent personalities from then and now eternalised in wax, and exhibited in appropriate settings. *Metro: de Brouckère/Beurs; Bus 29, 34, 47, 48, 60, 63, 65, 66, 95, 96; Tram 52, 55, 58, 81.*

Horta Museum, Rue Américaine/Amerikaansestraat 25. Tuesday to Sunday 2–5.30pm. Residence of the art nouveau architect Victor Horta. *Tram 81, 92; Bus 54, 60.*

Institute of Natural Sciences (Institut des Sciences Naturelles/Instituut voor Natuurwetenschapen), Rue Vautier/Vautierstraat 29. Tuesday to Sunday 9.30am–4.45pm. *Bus 34, 37, 38, 59, 80, 95, 96.*

Manneken Pis Wardrobe (Garderobe de Manneke Pis/De Klerenverzamerling van Manneke Pis). In the Municipal Museum (*see below*). Over 300 costumes.

Municipal Museum (Musée Communal de la Ville de Bruxelles/Stedelijk Museum van Brussel). Grand' Place/Grote Markt (Broodhuis/Maison du Roi). Monday, Tuesday, Wednesday, Friday 10am–12.30pm, 1.30–5pm, Thursday 10am–5pm, Saturday and Sunday 10am–1pm; closed on some holidays. Free admission on Sunday.

Municipal Museum of Woluwe-St Lambert (Musée Communal de Woluwe-St Lambert/Gemeentelijk Museum van Sint Lambrechts-Woluwe) Rue de la Charette/Karrestraat 40, St Lambrechts-Woluwe. July to September by appointment only; October to June Monday to Friday 9am–noon and 2–5pm. Exhibits depicting 19th-century life in Woluwe. *Bus 80.*

Museum of Art and History (Musée d'Art et d'Histoire/Museum voor Kunst en Geschiedenes). Parc du

The Manneken Pis Wardrobe

The Horta Museum

Cinquantenaire/Jubelpark 10. Tuesday to Friday 9.30am–12.25pm, 1.30–4.50pm, Saturday and Sunday 10am–12.30pm, 1.30–4.45pm; closed 1 January, 1 May, 1 and 11 November, 25 December. *Metro: Merode (line 1); Bus 20, 28, 36, 61, 67, 80; Tram 81.*

Museum of Central Africa

Museum of Central Africa (Musée de l'Afrique Centrale/Museum voor Midden-Afrika), Leuvensteenweg 13, Tervuren (13km/8 miles east of Brussels). 16 March to 15 October 9am–5.30pm; 16 October to 15 March 10am–4.30pm. *Tram 44.*

Museum of Costumes and Lace (Musée du Costume et de la Dentelle/Museum voor het kostuum en de kant), Rue de la Violette/Violetstraat 4–6. Monday, Tuesday, Wednesday, Friday 10am–12.30pm and 1.30–5pm, Thursday 10am–5pm, Saturday and Sunday 2–4.30pm. *Metro: Central Station; Tram 52, 55, 58, 81; Bus 29, 34, 47, 48, 63, 65, 66, 71, 95, 96.*

Museum of Fine Arts in Ixelles (Musée des Beaux-Arts d'Ixelles/Museum voor Schone Kunsten van Elsene), Rue Jan Van Volsem/JV Volsemstraat 71, Ixelles/Elsene. Tuesday to Friday 1–7.30pm, Saturday and Sunday 10am–5pm. Free admission except during special exhibitions. Works by Belgian artists including Magritte, Delvaux and De Smet; important collection of Toulouse-Lautrec posters. *Bus 37, 38, 71, 95, 96.*

Museum of Modern Art (Musée d'Art Moderne/Museum voor Moderne Kunst), Place Royale 1. Tuesday to Sunday 10am–1pm, 2–5pm. No admission charge. Paintings, sculptures, and prints from the 19th and 20th century. *Tram 92, 93, 94; Bus 20, 34, 38, 71, 95, 96.*

Museum of Musical Instruments (Musée Instrumental), Place du Petit Sablon/Kleine Zavel 17. The collection includes over 5,000 instruments from around the world. Tuesday, Thursday and Saturday 2.30–4.30pm, Wednesday 4–6pm, Sunday 10.30am–12.30pm. *Tram 92, 93, 94; Bus 20, 34, 71, 95, 96.*

Museum of Older Art

Museum of Older Art (Musée d'Art Ancien/Museum voor Oude Kunst), Rue de la Régence/Regentschapsstraat 3. Tuesday to Sunday 10am–noon, 1–5pm; closed 1 January, 1 May, 1 and 11 November, 25 December. Paintings, sculptures, drawings and tapestries from the 14th–18th century. *Tram 92, 93, 94; Bus 20, 34, 38, 71, 95, 96.*

Museum of Public Welfare (Musée de l'Assistance Publique/Museum van de Openbare Onderstand), Hôpital Saint Pierre/Sint Pieters Hospitaal, Rue Haute/Hoogstraat 298a, App. 1028. Wednesday 2–5pm; closed on public holidays. Life in Brussels and Brabant comes alive through this exhibition of furnishings and documents. *Metro: Hallepoort (line 2); Bus 20, 48.*

Waterloo Panorama Museum

Panorama Museum of Waterloo, Chemin des Vertes Bornes 90, Braine-l'Alleud/Eigenbrakel (18km/11 miles south of Brussels). Monday to Saturday 9.30am–6pm, Sunday and holidays 9.30am–6.30pm. Lion's Hill, Wax Museum, Wellington Museum, Ferme de Caillou. *Bus: line W of the SNCV from Gare du Midi.*

Planetarium, Avenue de Bouchout/Bouchoutlaan 10. Irregular opening times. Varying programmes in several languages. *Metro: Houba Brugmann (line 1A); Tram 18, 81; Bus H, WL, L, BW, LW.*

Postal Museum (Musée Postal), Place du Grand-Sablon/ Grote Zavel 40. Tuesday to Saturday 10am–4pm, Sunday and holidays 10am–12.30pm. A complete collection of Belgian stamps from 1845 to the present, plus the history of the postal, telephone and telegraph systems. *Tram 92, 93, 94; Bus 20, 34, 48, 95, 96.*

Postal Museum exhibit

Railway Museum (Musée du Chemin de Fer/Spoorwegmuseum). In North Station (Gare du Nord/Noordstation), entrance Rue du Progrès/Vooruitgangsstraat 76, St Joost. Monday to Friday 9am–4.30pm and on first Saturday of every month. *Metro: North Station; Tram 52, 55, 58, 81, 90; Bus 13, 37, 38, 47, 61, 97.*

Railway signals

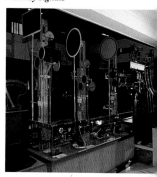

Rixensart Castle (southeast of Brussels, off the motorway to Namur). April to October daily except Friday 10am–noon and 2–6pm. The French gardens of this Renaissance castle were laid out by Le Nôtre.

Royal Palace (Palais Royal), Place des Palais/Paleizenplein. 30 July to 13 September Tuesday to Sunday 9.30am–3.30pm. *Tram: 92, 93, 94.*

Sound Museum (Musée de la Parole/Museum van de Stern). In the Albert I Library, 4 Bd. de l'Empereur. Open only by appointment. *Tram 92, 93, 94; Bus 20, 29, 34, 38, 48, 60, 63, 65, 71, 95, 96.*

Town Hall (Hôtel de Ville/Stadhuis), Grand' Place/Grote Markt. October to March Tuesday to Friday 9.30am–12.15pm, 1.45–5pm, Sunday and holidays 10am–noon, 2–4pm. The rooms house many reminders of the era when Brussels was the capital of the duchy of Brabant.

Tram Museum (Musée de Tram), Tervurenlaan 364b, St Pieters-Woluwe. Easter to beginning October: weekdays 1.30–7pm; Saturday, Sunday, holidays by appointment. The history of the tram from 1894–1935 is depicted in this museum. It contains 30 tram wagons. *Tram 39, 44; Bus 36, 42.*

Van Buuren Museum, Avenue Léo Errera/L Erreralaan 41, Ukkel. Monday, except January, 2–4pm and by appointment. Paintings and sculptures dating from the 16th–20th century exhibited in an interesting house dating from 1930.

Wiertz Museum, Rue Vautier/Vautierstraat 62. Tuesday to Sunday 10am–noon, 1–5pm. The former atelier of this Romantic painter houses a great number of his works. *Bus 20, 34, 80.*

Theatre and Music

The Theatre Toone

Opera House

With the wealth of theatres, night clubs and cultural centres in Brussels – over 40 such establishments – it is important to find out in plenty of time what is playing where during your stay in Brussels. A programme of events called *Balconop*, published by Brussels Tourist Information, lists forthcoming ballet, concerts and operas. This information office also sells tickets (11am–5pm) for some of the theatres *(see page 96)*. Tickets can also be obtained from BBB Agenda, rue du Chêne 10, 1000 Brussels, tel: 513 8946, 512 8277 or 513 8940.

The cream of the crop of Brussels theatres is the National Opera in the Théâtre Royal de la Monnaie, which stages operas and ballets. It is located near the Grand' Place, as are the smaller stages of Beursschouwburg, Théâtre de la Gaîte (operettas and musicals) and Théâtre des Galeries. Just outside the boulevard ring, to the north, is the Théâtre National de Belgique in the International Rogier Centre. To the northwest, just inside the ring road, is the Vlaamse Schouwburg and northeast of the Grand' Place is the Cirque Royal/Koninklijk Circus. In the Brussels Park, east of the Town Hall, is the Park Theatre and, finally, the Théâtre Molière is located to the southeast just outside the ring road.

A number of experimental theatres can be found in Brussels, although they often appear and disappear or change their names and addresses. One special attraction which should be mentioned is the renowned Toone VII Marionette Theatre near the Town Hall. It has been in operation since 1830. Folklore pieces for adults are performed every evening except Sunday. The repertoire changes monthly and the plays can usually be understood even by foreigners with no knowledge of the language.

Lovers of jazz will want to visit the following establishments: De Kaai, Quai aux Pierres de Taille, Le Mozart, Chaussée d'Alsemberg 541 (restaurant with live music), Bierodrome (at Place Fernand Cocq).

Cabaret and nightclubs

As the theatres empty after the last performance, the Brussels late-night establishments come to life. And the city has no dearth of these. Cabaret artists, illusionists or show masters are on hand to entertain. Musical variety acts, Brasilian shows, South American or Russian folklore and, of course, the famous transvestite shows can be found in the Belgian capital. Anyone seeking an evening of Brussels atmosphere will have no trouble finding a place to go. And when these clubs all close, there are always the discotheques as well as about 50 downtown restaurants which stay open into the small hours.

Late night-life

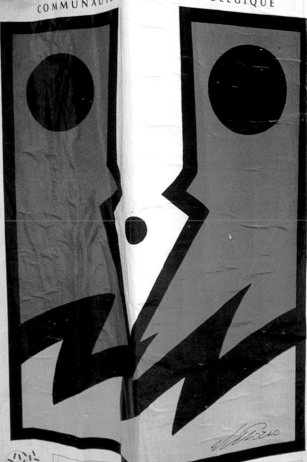

THEATRE NATIONALE

COMMUNAUTÉ FRANÇAISE DE BELGIQUE

jeu
ÉCRITURES

RENSEIGNEMENTS
ET LOCATION
02-217 03 03

Centre Rogier 1210 Bruxelles Tél. 02 217 81 ...

RENSEIGNEMENTS
ET LOCATION
02-217 03 03

jeu

Food and Drink

Opposite: an enticing display of food

Specialities of Brussels

Brussels offers a number of culinary specialities, including the following well-known dishes: Brussels chicory (rolled in ham or filled with ground meat); Brussels meat patties (small, lightly stewed, ground meat patties with chicory); green eel with herb sauce; *Choesels au Madère* (offal with Madeira sauce and champignons); Flemish *carbonade* (beef steamed in beer); Brussels sprouts (boiled then tossed in butter); and Brussels-style mussels, which are usually eaten with *pomme frites* (*see below*).

From the area around Brussels and just as highly recommended are: *Mechelen* asparagus (in a sauce of hard-boiled eggs, chopped parsley and melted butter, a real delicacy); poultry *Waterzooi* (chicken cooked in a vegetable broth and served in a cream sauce); jugged hare Flemish style (prepared with onions and served with stewed prunes).

Pommes frites or French fries: Anyone who thinks that *Frieten* are an invention of the fast food industry is mistaken. Although they have only gained such immense popularity in recent times, they were actually invented about 300 years ago in Liège and the surrounding area. They are available not only at snack stands on street corners but also as an accompaniment to a fine meal in the gourmet temples, and they are usually very good.

In addition to the wide variety of Belgian baked goods, the specialities of Brussels include: sugar cakes, rice cakes, raisin bread, *spekulatius* biscuits (spicy Christmas biscuits) and a variation called *pain d'armandes* (almond bread); and Brussels waffles (*gaufres*). Perhaps most importantly, Brussels is known as the world capital of pralines and chocolates.

85

Chocolates galore

The beverage menu

The national drink of Belgium is beer, brewed throughout the country in about 130 breweries. There are no less than 400 different kinds of beers and 200 different flavour variations. The beer of Ghent and Leuven are among the most famous, but the beers of Brussels are also renowned. Typical here is the natural fermentation process as, for instance, in *Faro* beer, a wheat beer brewed according to an ancient recipe. Also noteworthy is *Geuze-Lambic*, brewed from a mixture of half barley and half wheat. With a shot of *kirschwasser* added, it is known as *Kriek-Lambic*, and should definitely be sampled.

While the Belgians import most of their wine and cognac from France, many of the brandies and liqueurs are produced within Belgium.

Bringing the famous beer

Waterzooi

Restaurants for Gourmets

The Belgian capital boasts more than 1,800 restaurants. The Tourist Information Office in Brussels (*see page 97*) publishes a brochure annually with the title *Gourmet*, listing the addresses of the 300 most important establishments along with the opening times and prices. The critics employ a *fleur-de-lis* rating system to guide readers in their choice. A maximum of 5 *fleur-de-lis* may be awarded to what they consider to be the most distinguished restaurants in the city. This selection includes just a few of the best-known restaurants in Brussels which are of particular interest to the visitor, and where a meal is a true culinary experience.

Almost next door to each other in the vicinity of Koekelberg Basilika are a pair of celebrated restaurants bearing the names of their owner-chefs. **Bruneau**, owned by Jean-Pierre and Claire Bruneau (73–75 Avenue Broustin) is one of only three restaurants in the Brussels area to have been awarded the coveted three Michelin stars. **Dupont**, run by Claude Dupont and his wife (46 Avenue Vital-Riethuisen), has two. The specialities on offer in both these restaurants vary according to season and reflect the chefs' daily visits to the local market for fresh game, fine poultry, vegetables, salads and herbs. You are advised to reserve a table well in advance.

If you want divine style as well as superb cuisine head for **Comme Chez Soi** (23 Place Rouppe). Here Pierre Wynants, its owner-chef, serves three-star nouvelle cuisine specialities in an exquisite dining room with a belle-epoque atmosphere recalling the decorative style of Victor Horta, the famous Brussels architect of the 1920s and '30s.

Café life

Alternatively you might like to try **La Maison du Cygne** on the Grand' Place/Grote Markt 9l, lying at the very heart of the city. The entrance is discreetly tucked away in the Rue Charles Buls. It is a charming and elegant establishment and the perfect venue for a celebration dinner. To really make your meal an occasion, be sure to take an apéritif in the **Club Ommegang** beforehand.

At **L'Ecailler du Palais Royal** (18, Rue Bodenbroeck), René Falk and Attilio Basso are renowned for their exquisite seafood delicacies. Nowhere is the fish fresher or more skilfully prepared than here.

A popular haunt

Near the Bois de la Cambre stands the **Villa Lorraine** (75 Avenue du Vivier d'Or), for many years a favourite gourmet rendezvous. The setting is immaculate. Among Freddy van de Casserie's specialities are the incomparable 'Ecrivisses Villa Lorraine' – freshwater crayfish served with a sumptuous sauce of white wine and cream.

Pierre Romeyer serves particularly light, meticulously prepared dishes at his restaurant **Romeyer** (109 Chaussée de Groenendaal in Hoeilláart, 11 km/7 miles from Brussels). It isn't just the food which makes a visit to this restaurant so memorable. There can be few more idyllic spots on a summer evening than the terrace in front of Romeyer, overlooking its own gardens and private lake. Romeyer's philosophy, refreshingly self-effacing, is that a chef should adapt what he serves to meet the wishes of his customers, and not vice versa. The presentation, harmony of taste and variety of his specialities are equally highly commended. Of particular note are the home-made pâtisseries.

87

The outskirts of Brussels are also blessed with a number of first-class restaurants, including **De Bijgaarden** (20, I. Van Beverenstraat) in Grand-Bigard (7 km/4 miles northeast of the capital), **Le Trèfle à Quatre** in Genval (87, Avenue du Lac) and **Barbizon** in Jezus-Eik (95, Welriekendedreef).

Cafés, bistros and bars

No city is complete without a wide-ranging choice of cafés, bistros and bars; Brussels is no exception. The district surrounding the Grand' Place/Grote Markt is particularly well endowed with places serving good food at inexpensive prices. In some of the narrow alleys hereabouts it seems as if every house has been converted into a restaurant of some kind. A typical example is Rue des Bouchers/Beenhouwersstraat where, in many cases, polished antique barrows and shelves laden with the ingredients of house specialities are placed in front of the restaurants to tempt passers-by. When business is slack, waiters and chefs often come out and stand in front of their restaurants to drum up trade. Don't be shy of accepting their invitations. Such fare is typically Belgian and rea-

Chips with everything

sonably priced. The district as a whole is known as the city's 'stomach'. It is a fitting description, but you will find more than just places to eat. You will also find originality and a loving regard for centuries-old traditions.

One of the most atmospheric places to eat in town is **Toone VII** (located at Impasse Schuddevelt 6, Petite Rue des Bouchers) – an old inn containing a puppet theatre, which is reached via a claustrophobically narrow passageway between two houses. The theatre (go up the rickety stairs) stages performances of classical plays such as *Hamlet* and *Faust*, interspersed by personal comments on the plot by Toone, a true Brussels character, whose remarks lighten the tragic action on the stage. The puppet theatre/restaurant has been a feature of Brussels for several generations.

Have some ice-cream
Waiters often tout for trade

The majority of bars and bistros cannot provide such original entertainment, but most of them offer at least a welcoming atmosphere. The décor, usually of a rustic nature and bearing the patina of age, radiates a relaxing ambience. The walls, stucco and beams of such place are invariably brown with generations of tobacco smoke.

Like the French, the citizens of Brussels enjoy sitting at a table on the pavement in front of the restaurant or bar. Even in the sheltered, air-conditioned shopping galleries customers display a marked preference for outside tables. Here you will usually find coffee and a selection of tempting cakes and pastries on offer.

Elsewhere in the city, cafés-cum-pâtisseries tend to be thin on the ground. There are some excellent cake shops – **Wittamer**, on the Place du Grand Sablon, is one of the continent's best – but hardly any are attached to an attractive café of the type common in Germany or Austria. Occasionally you may come across a shabbily furnished room in a department store, where a cup of coffee and biscuits are served – or, if you are lucky, a so-called 'Tearoom', where cakes and other sweet specialities are available.

The Boulevard du Midi/Zuidlaan is quite different. Here, in the **Café Strauss**, you can partake of excellent Black Forest cherry gâteau or an apple cake which tastes home-made in Berlin. German coffee is also served here.

Another excellent pâtisserie is in the Upper Town in the Avenue Louise/Louizalaan: **Nihoul** has a salon serving a wide variety of cakes, as well as a wide range of snacks and salads.

Within the Galerie du Sablon on the square of the same name you will not find a café as such; there is, however, a very attractive restaurant: **Les Jardins du Sablon**. It is an ideal setting for recouping one's strength after the rigours of exploring the many interesting shops in this part of Brussels.

Shopping

A shopping spree in Brussels can be a true delight. The wide array of shopping centres, markets and speciality shops will please even the most discerning tourist.

The city is justifiably famous for its diamonds, lace, and fine, hand-made chocolates, but there are many other goods worth buying. Brussels is an Eldorado for comic freaks. A number of bookshops offer both new and used comics, reading rooms, and evening as well as Sunday opening hours. A few addresses: **Fil à Terre**, Waversesteenweg 198 (reading room); **Schlirf Book**, Waterloosesteenweg 752 (also open Sunday); **Le Depot**, Zuidstraat 108 (for both new and used books). For fans of printed matter, books, postcards, posters and more, the Royal Army Museum is the place to be on the first Saturday of every month.

Bookshop

The most important shopping centres in the Old Town are **City II**, a three-floor mall on Nieuwstraat and the **Anspach Centre** on Anspachlaan. Shop like a prince in the glass-covered arcades of the Galerie du Roi, Galerie de la Reine and the Galerie des Princes, all of which together form the **Galeries Saint-Hubert**. This arcade, built in 1846, is famous as the first of its kind in Europe.

Antique silver

Brussels has fashion as well as food: Gucci, Versaci and Nina Ricci can all be found in the decidedly upmarket Boulevard de Waterloo.

Markets

The city offers a market for every taste. The most popular are, without a doubt, the antique and flea markets. Most are held either on Saturday or Sunday.

Antique Market, Grand Sablon (Grote Zavel), Saturday 9am–6pm, Sunday 9am–2pm.

Flower Market, Grand' Place (Grote Markt), daily 8am–6pm.

Bouquet from the Flower Market

Bird Market, Grand' Place (Grote Markt), Sunday 7am–2pm.

Flea Market, Place du Jeu de Balle (Vossenplein), daily 7am–2pm.

Food and Textile Market, Place Bara (Gare du Midi/Zuidstation), Sunday 5am–1pm.

Even for those who have no intention of buying a horse, a visit to the **horse market**, where deals are sealed with a handshake, is an experience not to be missed. A large one takes place every Sunday from 7am–2pm in Zuidlaan. In Molenbeek, at Herzogin-von-Brabantplein, the horse market is held every Friday from 5am–noon.

The TIB (*see page 97*) can provide further information about all markets in and around Brussels, including the food and mixed wares markets.

89

The North Station

Leuven Town Hall

Preceding pages:
one way of getting around

Getting There

By plane

Most major airlines including Sabena, the Belgian national carrier, fly to Brussels-Zaventem which lies some 15km (9 miles) from the city centre. A rail service operates every 20 minutes (5.39am–11.14pm) between the airport and the Gare du Nord in the city centre, the journey takes 20 minutes. Trains also run to the other stations. There is an hourly bus service from each of the stations. Buses also serve Antwerp (50 minutes) and Liège (90 minutes). Airport tax is included in the air fare.

In the UK: Sabena, 177 Piccadilly, London W1 (within the Air France office, for personal callers), reservations tel: 0181-780 1444.

In the US: Sabena, 720 Fifth Avenue (on the 5th floor), Manhattan, New York 10019, tel: 212-247 8390.

By train

Numerous international railway lines pass through Brussels. There are regular international services from Paris, Amsterdam, Cologne, Ostend and Zeebrugge, the latter two connecting with car-ferry or jetfoil services from Britain. The direct rail service from London to Brussels through the Channel Tunnel is operated by Eurostar (tel: 44-1233 617575 from abroad; 0345 881 881 from within the UK). The journey time is 3 hours.

Those wishing to make excursions from Brussels into the outlying areas should consider purchasing the tourist ticket B-Tourrail. It is valid throughout the entire railway network for five days within a 17-day period. The ticket is issued either for first- or second-class travel. Children under six travel free while older children and young people receive considerable discounts. The TTB ticket is similar to the B-Tourrail but is also valid for bus, tram and metro transportation.

Travel time from Brussels is 20 minutes to Leuven or Mechelen, 30 minutes to Antwerp or Ghent, 50 minutes to Namur, 60 minutes to Tournai, 65 minutes to Liège and 75 minutes to Ostende.

Some special offers:

Network ticket: this is valid for 16 consecutive days. Allows travel throughout Belgium by any means of transportation.

Half-fare privilege ticket: this affords a 50 percent discount for a period of one month throughout the entire railway network.

Senior citizens discount: senior citizens holding a Rail-Europ Senior Ticket receive 50 percent discount on rail travel throughout Belgium.

Weekend ticket: reduced price ticket valid from noon on Friday until noon on Monday. Small groups receive a 60 percent discount.

Additionally, it is possible to book day trips with or without supplementary bus excursions. Information about these offers can be obtained at larger railway stations (tel: 219 2640) as well as at the Belgian Railway Association (SNCB/NMBS).

By car

Brussels, one of Western Europe's traffic hubs, has a superb motorway network. The E19 comes in from Paris 310km (193 miles) to the southeast and, via Antwerp, from Amsterdam 232km (144 miles) to the north; the E40 comes in via Ghent from Ostend and Zeebrugge 114km (71 miles) to the west and, via Liège and Leuven, from Cologne 228km (142 miles) to the east; the E411 arrives, via Namur, from Luxembourg 220km (137 miles) to the southeast. All motorways converge on the motorway ring about 10km (6 miles) outside the city centre.

The fastest means of getting from the UK to Belgium by car is with Le Shuttle (tel: 0990 353535), the Channel Tunnel service taking cars and their passengers from Folkestone to Calais on a drive-on-drive-off system. In summer there are up to four trains an hour.

A driver's licence, vehicle registration papers and a nationality sticker on the rear of the vehicle are necessary when entering Belgium. The speed limit is 60km/h (35mph) within a town and 120km/h (70mph) on the motorway or 4-lane highways. On all other roads it is 90km/h (55mph). In Belgium the rule of right-of-way for those on the right is valid, with very few exceptions. These exceptions are always clearly marked by traffic signs. Hitchhiking is forbidden on the motorway.

Emergencies: in case of an accident with personal injury, call the emergency number 100 to request help. This number is valid throughout the country. Brussels emergency service: RACB day and night, tel: 736 5959. TCB from 7am–11pm, tel: 233 2211.

Automobile clubs: Royal Automobil Club de Belgique (RACB), Aarlenstraat 53, B-1040 Brussels, tel: 736 5959; Touring Club Royal de Belgique (TCB), 44 rue de la Loi, B-1040 Brussels, tel: 233 2211.

By sea

Ostend and Zeebrugge are Belgium's two car-ferry terminals (Ostend also for the jetfoil), with connections from the British ports of Dover, Harwich and Hull (for Zeebrugge only). It is also possible to travel from Britain to ports such as Calais and Vlissingen and then by motorway to Brussels.

Traffic on the Boulevard Ring

93

Keeping to the speed limit

Getting Around

Parking

Parking in Brussels is regulated partially by the use of parking meters and partially by the use of zones requiring a parking card. Garage parking is available in the city centre. Be sure to take note of the closing times.

Brussels public transport network is run by several different companies. It is a system which is not always easy for the foreign visitor to understand.

City railway

Among the stations and stops of the SNCB (Sociéte Nationale des Chemins Fers Belges), those most important for the tourist are the ones of the north–south underground line (Pré-Metro line 3 and tram lines 51, 55, 58, 81 and 90). These run through the city centre between North Station (Gare du Nord/Noordstation) and South Station (Gare

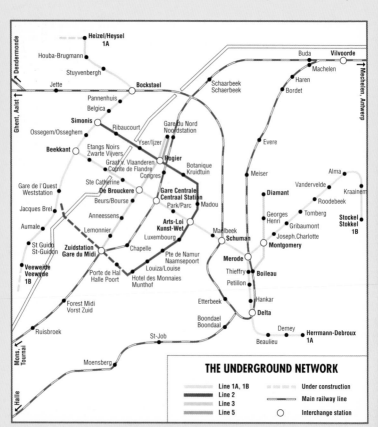

THE UNDERGROUND NETWORK

Line 1A, 1B	Under construction
Line 2	Main railway line
Line 3	
Line 5	Interchange station

du Midi/Zuidstation). The most important stops are Congrès, Central Station (Gare Centrale/Centraal Station) and Chapelle/Kapellekerk. Note that a transfer is possible, at Place de Brouckère, to the Metro lines 1A-B and at Place Rogier to Pré-Metro line 2. The SNCB also serves Greater Brussels with about 20 suburban stations.

Underground (Metro)

The Brussels underground network consists of two underground lines (with a length of about 33km/20 miles) which connect the eastern and western parts of the city.

The underground network is supplemented by three Pré-Metro lines. Pré-Metro means that the completed underground tracks are also used at the present time by the trams of the STIB (Sociéte des Tramways Intercommunaux de Bruxelles).

The underground lines are as follows:

Metro 1A

Underground travel

This line runs west of the city centre in a north–south direction before crossing through the city centre and the Quartier Léopold in an east–west direction. The stations are: Heysel (Atomium), Houba-Brugman, Stuyvenbergh, Bockstael (near Parc de Laeken), Pannenhuis, Belgica, Simonis, Osseghem/Ossegem, Beekkant, Etangs Noirs/Zwarte Vijvers, Comte de Flandre/Graaf van Vlaanderen, St Catherine, de Brouckère (interchange with line 3), Gare Centrale/Centraal Station, Parck/Park, Arts-Loi/Kunst-Wet, Maelbeek, Schumann, Merode, Thieffry, Petillon, Hankar, Delta, Beaulieu, Demey, Hermann/Debroux.

Metro 1B

This line runs west of the city centre before crossing through the city and the Quartier Leopold in an east–west direction. The stations are: Veeweyde, St Guidon, Aumale, Jacques Brel, Gare de l'Ouest/West Station, Beekkant. Here it joins the line 1A until Merode. At that station, the Metro 1B branches to the northeast, stopping at the following stations: Montgomery, Josephine Charlotte, Gribaumont, Tomberg, Roodebeek, Vandervelde, Alma, Kraainem, Stokkel.

Pré-Metro line 2 (Trams 2, 18, 19, 32, 101, 103)

This follows the course of the boulevard ring along its northeastern and eastern sectors, with the following stations: Simonis, Ribaucourt, Yser, Rogier, Botanique/Kruidtuin, Madou, Arts-Loi/Kunst-Wet (transfer station with Metro 1A–B), Luxembourg, Porte de Namur/Naamse Poort, Place Louise/Louizaplein, Hotel des Monnaies, Munthof, Porte de Hal/Hallepoort, and Zuidstation/Gare du Midi.

Pre-Metro line 3 (Trams 52, 55, 58, 81 and 90)
This north–south line crosses through the city centre following the large boulevards. The stations are: Gare du Nord/Noordstation, Rogier (interchange with line 2), de Brouckère (interchange with Metro 1A–B), Bourse/Beurs, Anneessens, Lemonnier, Gare du Midi/Zuidstation.

Pre-Metro line 5 (Trams 23 and 90)
This north–south line runs east of the city centre along the 'middle' ring road, linking the boroughs of Schaerbeek/Schaarbeek and Etterbeek. The stations are: Bd A Reyers, Diamant, Georges Henri, Montgomery (interchange with the Metro 1B), Boileau.

Art in the Metro
Contemporary Belgian artists have transformed the underground stations into veritable galleries of art. The TIB (*see page 97*) and the Information Office of the STIB have a free brochure about art in the Metro. Special conducted tours are also available. For more information, contact TIB.

City tram

Bus

The STIB has about 30 bus and tram lines (two-digit numbers) covering the city. The buses of the SNCV (Sociéte Nationale des Chemins de Fer Vicinaux), which has about 70 bus lines, carry a three-digit number plus one or two letters. They depart mainly from the North Station and from Place Rouppe in the south of the city centre.

Tickets

The STIB tourist ticket is good for unlimited travel within a 24-hour period. It can be purchased at the reception of the TIB (Brussels Tourist Office), the Town Hall, Grand' Place/Grote Markt, at the Metro information offices or at the railway stations.

Single tickets are available as well as tickets for five or 10 trips. They can be purchased from the driver, at the ticket windows and automatic ticket machines in the Metro stations and in some stationery shops. Tickets must be stamped by the automatic ticket punchers before boarding. These are found at the entrances to underground stations as well as at the bus stops. A transfer from the tram or Metro to a bus costs extra.

Red and white or blue and white signs mark the tram and bus stops. The underground stations are marked by a large white M on a blue background.

City tours

During the summer months, some travel agencies offer daily conducted tours of the city in various languages. Brussels Tourist Office, tel: 513 8940 and 513 9090.

Tourist bus

Facts for the Visitor

Visas

Citizens of the European Community and some other European countries do not need a passport but they must have an ID card; in the case of UK citizens this would have to be a British Visitors' Passport. Citizens of the EC, most other European countries, the USA, Australia, Canada, Japan and some other countries, do not require a visa. If in doubt, check with the Belgian consulate in your country of origin, or with your travel agent or air carrier.

Customs

Non-EC members can bring 400 cigarettes, one bottle of spirits, two of wine and 50g of perfume; EC-members have guide levels of 800 cigarettes, 10 litres of spirit and 90 litres of wine. Customs keep a close watch for drugs, which are illegal.

Currency regulations

There is neither a limit nor a declaration requirement for travellers cheques and the like. There is no limit on the import and export of foreign currency. A maximum of 7,000 francs will be paid on a Eurocheque.

97

Information

TIB office

In the UK: Belgian Tourist Office, Premier House, Gayton Road, Harrow, Middlesex, tel: 081-861 3300.

In the US: Belgian Tourist Office, 745 Fifth Avenue, New York 10151, tel: 212-758 8130.

In Brussels: TIB (Tourist Information Brussels) in the Town Hall, Grand' Place/Grote Markt, tel: 513 8940.

Brussels for young people

Those planning a stay in Brussels should pick up a copy

Fun for the young

of the Belgium guide *Use It* which contains many helpful hints and addresses. It is available at the Belgian Tourist office. The weekly English-language magazine, *The Bulletin*, is also a valuable source of information.

Currency and exchange

The Belgian unit of currency is the Belgian franc (bfr) = 100 centimes (c). Notes for 5,000, 1,000, 500, 100 and 50 francs as well as 20, 10, 5 and 1 franc coins and 50 and 25 centime pieces are in circulation. Currency can be exchanged in all banks during normal opening hours (generally 9am–noon and 2–4pm). Additionally, the exchange offices in the North and South stations are open daily from 7am–11pm and in the Central Station from 8.45am–5.20pm. An automatic exchange machine can be found in the Brussels Tourist Office at Grasmarkt/Rue du Marché aux Herbes 61. It can exchange five different currencies into Belgian francs.

Lace shop

Opening times

Shops are normally open Monday to Saturday from 9am–6pm, although some of them close on Monday. There are few late-night shops, but the neighbourhood 'corner store' may be open until 9pm. On Friday department stores and other shops stay open until 9pm.

Public holidays

Aside from the main religious holidays and 1 May (Labour Day), Belgium celebrates its national holiday on 21 July, Armistice Day on 11 November, Assumption of the Virgin on 15 August and All Saints' Day on 1 November. If one of these celebrations falls on a Sunday, the following day is a bank holiday.

Postal delivery

Post

The post offices are normally open Monday to Friday from 9am–5pm. Some offices are open on Friday evening and Saturday morning. The post office at Gare du Midi (Avenue Fosny) is also open at weekends, during holidays and at night.

Telephone

The telephone rates are posted in the telephone booths. Before placing a call you should have plenty of 5 and 20 franc coins. It is easier to use the telecard (with 20 units), which can be obtained at any post office. To make an international call, dial 00 followed by the code of the country: Australia 61; France 33; Germany 49; Japan 81; Netherlands 31; Spain 34; United Kingdom 44; US and Canada 1. The country code for Belgium (from the UK) is 010 32; the city code for Brussels is 02.

Time

Belgium is six hours ahead of US Eastern Standard Time and one hour ahead of Greenwich Mean Time.

The Clock Museum

Climate

Most of Belgium has a mild climate with relatively cool summers and mild winters. Only the climate in the Ardennes is influenced by the continental conditions. Here, there is about 1,000 mm (39 ins) of rain fall as opposed to about 800mm (31 ins) in Brussels.

Voltage

The voltage is 220 volts AC.

Medical

Visitors from the EC have the right to claim health services which are available to Belgians. UK visitors should obtain Form E111 from the Department of Health prior to departure. Non-EC citizens should definitely have a travellers' health insurance policy. Information can be obtained at travel agencies or private insurance companies.

Standby doctors: available 24 hours a day, tel: 479 1818 or 648 8000.

Standby dentists: Monday to Saturday 9pm–7am and Saturday 7am to Monday 7am, tel: 426 1026 or 428 5888.

Ambulances (for non-emergencies): available 24 hours a day, tel: 649 1122.

Emergencies

Emergency, ambulance and fire brigade, tel: 100.
Police and Gendarmerie, tel: 101.
(Police, other), tel: 513 2840.

Calling home

Lost property offices

Aircraft: arrivals hall, tel: 723 6011.
Visitors' hall, tel: 722 3940.
Train: for Brussels, tel: 219 2880.
Public transportation: tel: 515 2394.

Foreigners in need

Bruxelles Accueil (in several languages), 6 rue de Tabora, tel: 511 2715, 511 8178.
SOS Youth, tel: 512 9020, day and night.
Emergency welfare, tel: 425 5725.

Diplomatic missions

UK, Rue Joseph II 28, Etterbeck, tel: 217 9000.
US, Boulevard de Regent 27, tel: 513 3830.
Canada, Avenue de Telvarel 2, tel: 735 6040.
Australia, Avenue des Arts 52, tel: 213 0500.
Ireland, Rue du Luxembourg 19, tel: 513 6633.

No shortage of rooms

Accommodation

The TIB (Tourist Information Bruxelles/Brussel) in the Town Hall at Grand' Place can provide information on hotel rooms. It is open daily during the summer season 9am–6pm (closed Saturday 15 December to Easter). The service can be reached by phone daily from 9am–6pm, tel: 02-513 8940, fax: 02-514 4538.

Hotel rooms can be reserved at short notice through the BTR (Belgium Tourist Reservations), either in writing, by fax or by phone. Address: PO Box 41, B-1000 Brussels 23, tel: 02-230 5029, fax: 02-230 6019. Remember to give the exact date of arrival and departure, number of persons, price category, with or without bath/shower. The listing below starts with the luxury price category.

Hotels
$$$$$ – $$$$
Amigo, Rue de L'Amigo/Vriendstaat 1–3, tel: 511 5910 (183 rooms); **Brussels Europa**, Rue de la Loi/Wetstraat 107, tel: 230 1333 (245 rooms); **Brussels Hilton**, Boulevard de Waterloo/Waterloolaan 38, tel: 513 8877 (373 rooms); **Brussels President**, Avenue Louise/Louizalaan 319, tel: 640 2415 (44 rooms); **Copthorne Stéphanie**, Avenue Louise/Louizalaan 91–3, tel: 539 0240 (142 rooms); **Jolly Hotel Sablon**, Place du Grand Sablon/Grote Zavel, tel: 217 0120 (203 rooms); **Mayfair**, Avenue Louise/Louizalaan 381–3, tel: 649 9800 (95 rooms); **Métropole**, Place de Brouckère/De Brouckèreplein 31, tel: 217 2300 (410 rooms); **Palace**, Rue Gineste/Ginestestraat 3, tel: 217 6200 (360 rooms); **Président World Trade**

Centre, Bd E Jacqmain/E Jacqmainlaan 180, tel: 217 2020 (310 rooms); **Ramada**, Chaussée de Charleroi/Steenweg op Charleroi 38, tel: 539 3000 (202 rooms); **SAS Royal Hotel**, Rue du Fossé-aux-Loups/Wolvengracht 47, tel: 511 8888 (281 rooms); **Scandic Crown Hotel**, Rue Royale/Koningstraat 250, tel: 217 1234 (325 rooms); **Sheraton**, Manhattan Center, Place Rogier/Rogierplein, tel: 219 3400 (476 rooms); **Sofitel Brussels**, Avenue de la Toisson d'Or/Guldenvlieslaan 40, tel: 725 1160 (125 rooms); **Sodehotel De Woluwe**, Avenue E Mournier/Mournierlaan 5, tel: 775 2111 (120 rooms); **Tagawa**, Avenue Louise/Louizalaan 321–5, tel: 640 8029 (76 rooms).

$$$

Agenda, Rue de Florence/Florencestraat 6, tel: 539 0031 (38 rooms); **Alfa Louise**, Rue Blanche/Blanchestraat 4, tel: 537 9210 (83 rooms); **Arcade Sainte Catherine**, Rue Joseph Plateau/Jozef Plateaustraat 2, tel: 513 7620 (234 rooms); **Argus**, Rue Capitaine Crespel/Kapitein Crespelstraat 6, tel: 514 0770; **Bedford**, Rue du Midi/Zuidstraat 135, tel: 512 7840 (220 rooms); **Cascade**, Rue de la Source/Bronstraat 14, tel: 230 2135 (42 rooms); **Chambord**, Rue de Namur/Naamsestraat 82, tel: 513 4119 (69 rooms); **Charlemagne**, Bd Charlemagne/Karel de Grotelaan 25, tel: 230 2135 (66 rooms); **City Garden**, Rue Joseph II/Joseph II-Straat 59, tel: 230 0945 (96 rooms); **Colonies**, Rue de Croisades/Kruisvaartenstraat 8, tel: 217 0094 (100 rooms); **Delta**, Chaussée de Charleroi/Steenweg op Charleroi 17, tel: 539 0160 (246 rooms); **Diplomat**, Rue Jean Stas/Jan Stasstraat 32, tel: 537 4250 (68 rooms); **Manos**, Chaussée de Charleroi/Steenweg op Charleroi 100–4, tel: 539 0250 (38 rooms); **Fimhotel Expo**, Avenue Impératrice Charlotte/Keizerin Charlottelaan 6, tel: 478 7080 (80 rooms); **Ibis Brussels Centre**, Rue du Marché aux Herbes/Grasmarkt 100, tel: 514 4040 (170 rooms); **New Siru**, Place Rogier/Rogierplein, tel: 217 7580 (103 rooms); **Oxford**, Avenue de Jette/Jetselaan 228, 1090 Heysel/Heysel, tel: 424 3011; **Scheers**, Boulevard Adolphe Max/Adolphe Maxlaan 132, tel: 217 7760 (62 rooms).

$$

Auberge St-Michel, Grand'Place/Grote Markt 15, tel: 511 0956 (15 rooms); **Congrès**, Rue du Congrès/Congresstraat 42–4, tel: 217 1890 (38 rooms); **Continental**, Place de la Constitution/Grondwetplein 18, tel: 538 0364 (48 rooms); **Derby**, Avenue de Tervuren/Tervurenlaan 24, tel: 733 0819 (30 rooms); **Gascogne**, Boulevard Adolphe Max/Adolphe Maxlaan 137, tel: 217 6962 (18 rooms); **Georges V**, Rue 't Kint/Kintstraat 23, tel: 513 5093 (17 rooms); **Grande Cloche**, Place Rouppe/Rouppeplein 10,

Mutual attraction

Belgian rooftops

tel: 512 6140 (45 rooms); **La Potiniére**, Rue FJ Navez/FJ Navezstraaat 165, tel: 215 2030 (37 rooms); **Madeleine**, Rue de la Montagne/Bergstraat 24, tel: 513 2675 (28 rooms); **Mirabeau**, Place Fontainas/Fontainasplein 18–20, tel: 511 1972 (29 rooms); **Queen Anne**, Boulevard Emile Jacqmain/Emile Jacqmainlaan 110, tel: 217 1600 (237 rooms); **Prince de Liège**, Chaussée de Ninove/Ninoofsteenweg 662–4, tel: 523 1815 (23 rooms); **Ravensteinhof**, Chaussée de Ninove/Ninoofsteenweg 685, tel: 522 6868 (18 rooms); **Van Belle**, Chausée de Mons/Bergensteenweg 39–45, tel: 521 3516 (84 rooms); **Windsor**, Place Rouppe/Rouppeplein 13, tel: 511 2014.

Guesthouses

$$

Trois Tilleuls, Berensheide 8, tel: 672 3014 (8 rooms); **Vielle Laterne**, Rue des Grans Carmes/Lievevrouwbroerstraat 29, tel: 512 7494 (6 rooms).

$

Résidence Sabina, Rue du Nord/Noordstraat 78, tel: 218 2637; **Bosquet**, Rue Bosquet/Bosquetstraat 70, tel: 538 5230. **Welcome**, 5 Rue du Peuplier, tel: 219 9546.

Staying with a local family

In addition to guest-houses, there is the possibility of bed-and-breakfast type accommodation with a local family. There are single or double rooms with shared or private bathrooms, and breakfast is included in the price. Such accommodation can be booked through La Rose de Vents/De Windroos, 1A Avenue de Deminieurs, 1090 Brussels, tel: 02-425 4071, fax: 02-425 3561.

Hotels in the surrounding area

Beersel (12km/7miles southwest): **$$$ Centre**, Ukkelseweg 121, tel: 02-376 2615 (12 rooms).

Diegem (9km/6 miles northeast): **$$$$ Holiday Inn**, Brussels Airport, Holidaystraat 7, tel: 02-720 5865 (300 rooms); **$$$$ Novotel**, Brussels Airport, Olmenstraat 1, tel: 02-720 5830 (158 rooms); **$$$$ Fimhotel**, Brussels Airport, Berkenlaan, tel: 02-720 4801 (79 rooms).

Overijse (17km/11 miles southeast): **$$$ Panorama**, Hengstenbergstraat 73, tel: 02- 687 7198 (44 rooms).

Ruisbroek (9km/6 miles southwest): **$$$$ Budget Motel Total-Jacques Borel**, Paris-Brussels road, tel: 02-377 1156 (60 rooms).

Strombeek-Bever (9km/6 miles north): **$$$ Pére Boudart**, Romeinsweg 592, tel: 02-478 1196 (41 rooms); **$$ Strombeek**, Temselaan 6, tel: 02-478 8367 (12 rooms); **$$ Château d'Eau**, Romeinsweg 578, tel: 02-478 2499 (12 rooms).

Zaventem (12km/7 miles northeast): **$$$ Hôtel-Résidence Z**, Kerkplein 19, tel: 02-720 6391 (8 rooms).

Youth and student accommodation

Youth Hostel Brueghel, Hoek Keizerslaan–Rue du Saint-Esprit/Heilige-Geeststraat 2, tel: 511 0436.

Auberge de Jeunesse Jacques Brel, Rue de la Sablonnière/Zavelputstraat 30, tel: 218 0187 (facilities for disabled people are available).

Maison Internationale, Chaussée de Wavre/Waversesteenweg 205, tel: 648 8529.

Auberge de Jeunesse Jean Nihon, Rue de l'Eléphant/Olifantstraat 4, 1080 Molenbeek-St Jean/St Jans-Molenbeek, tel: 215 3100.

Centre Internationale Etudiants Tiers-Monde, Rue de Parme/Parmastraat 26, St-Gilles, tel: 02/537 8961.

Youth Hostel Centre of Greater Brussels, Rue Traversière/Dwarsstraat 8, tel: 217 0158.

Sleep Well Auberge du Marais, Rue de la Blanchisserie/Blekerijstraat 27, tel: 218 5050.

Foyer Protestant International **David Livingstone**, Avenue Coghen 119, 1180 Uccle/Ukkel (males only), tel: 343 3089.

Seeking accommodation

103

Campsites

There are no camp-grounds in Brussels itself. The nearest ones in the province of Brabant are in Huizingen (15km/9 miles southwest), Neerijse (20km/13 miles east) and Wezembeek-Oppem (14km/8 miles east).

Index